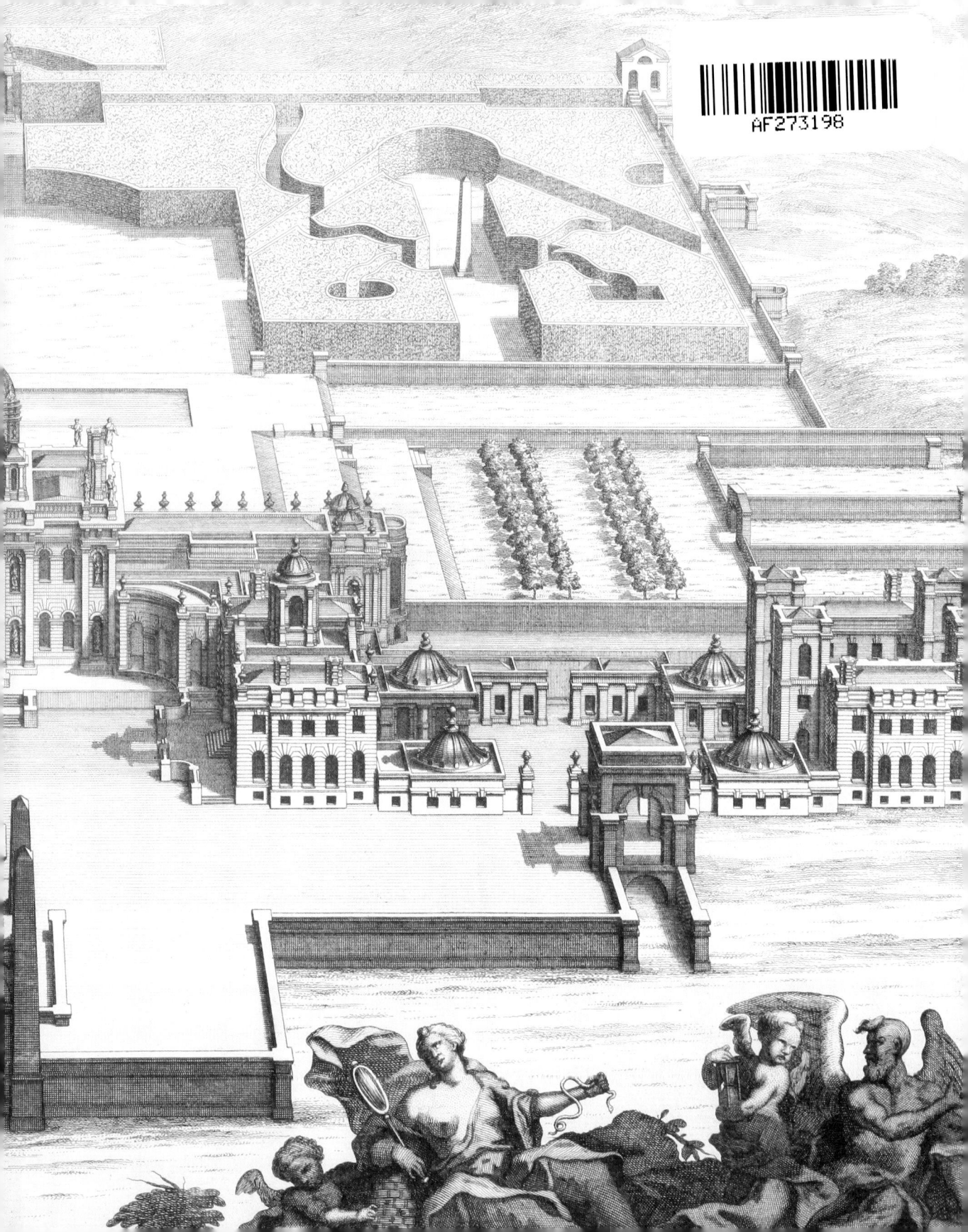

Castle Howard

Christopher Ridgway

CASTLE HOWARD

SCALA ARTS & HERITAGE PUBLISHERS

Castle Howard

'Nobody ... had informed me that I should at one view see a palace, a town, a fortified city, temples on high places, woods worthy of being each a metropolis of the Druids, vales connected to hills by other woods, the noblest lawn in the world fenced by half the horizon, and a mausoleum that would tempt one to be buried alive. In short I've seen gigantic places before, but never a sublime one.'

HORACE WALPOLE, 1772

Contents

Castle Howard has been home to the Howard family since the day it was built, more than 300 years ago. Successive generations have welcomed visitors through its doors and today it is your continuing support that enables the endless task of restoration and renovation. The hands of countless craftsmen and artists have come together here over the years, creating what is, in itself, a work of art. We hope that, in visiting Castle Howard and in reading this book, you will enjoy both their exquisite work and the vision of our eighteenth-century ancestors, along with continuing contributions from the present day.

The Howards of Castle Howard

The Howard family can trace its ancestry back to Thomas Howard, 3rd Duke of Norfolk, who served Henry VIII as a courtier and a military commander. He was most famous for supplying the king with two of his six wives: his nieces Anne Boleyn and Katherine Howard. The duke survived the ruthless world of Tudor court politics, albeit not before he had endured a near brush with death, escaping the executioner's axe only because the king had died the night before he was due to be beheaded.

As with all large families, over the years it divided into multiple branches, and the Castle Howard roots lie with the 3rd Duke's great-grandson, Lord William Howard of Naworth Castle, Cumbria. At the end of the sixteenth century Castle Howard had not been dreamt of, let alone built, but among Lord William's extensive land holdings in the north of England was an estate in Yorkshire that would in time become the base for his descendants.

BELOW LEFT Thomas Howard, 3rd Duke of Norfolk, studio of Hans Holbein the Younger, c.1542.

BELOW RIGHT Charles Howard, 1st Earl of Carlisle, by Sir Godfrey Kneller, c.1680.

ABOVE LEFT Edward Howard, 2nd Earl of Carlisle, by Sir Godfrey Kneller, c.1690.

ABOVE RIGHT Charles Howard, 3rd Earl of Carlisle, by William Aikman, 1728.

His great-grandson Charles Howard was an adept politician and successful soldier who negotiated the conflicting loyalties of the English Civil War, managing to serve under Oliver Cromwell and also emerge unscathed at the Restoration of the monarchy in 1660, to be created 1st Earl of Carlisle by Charles II in 1661.

His son Edward, the 2nd Earl, was elected Whig MP for Morpeth in 1666 and was later made Governor of Carlisle but outlived his father by only seven years. He married Elizabeth Uvedale and of their six children only one, Charles, survived to maturity, inheriting the title in 1692.

As a young man the 3rd Earl was the first member of the family to make a Grand Tour, journeying to Italy in 1688. A decade later, as his political career began to flourish, he decided to consolidate his position as a land-owning grandee in Yorkshire and build a magnificent new mansion at the ancient

BELOW LEFT Frederick
Howard, 5th Earl of
Carlisle, by John Hoppner,
c.1790.

BELOW RIGHT Caroline,
5th Countess of Carlisle,
by Sir Joshua Reynolds,
1770–72.

family seat of Henderskelfe. This was a sleepy settlement consisting of an old castle, a church and a few dwellings, all of which were to vanish with the building of Castle Howard.

His marriage to Anne Capel, daughter of the Earl of Essex, produced five children, but by the early 1700s the marriage had begun to fail as Charles became enamoured by something else: his grand project, the creation of Castle Howard. By 1704 husband and wife were on the verge of separating. Anne left Yorkshire and Charles largely abandoned London.

Henry, the 4th Earl, devoted his life to connoisseurship and assembling art collections. Such was his reputation that the author Horace Walpole described him as a 'great virtuoso'. Henry first visited Italy in 1714–15, becoming a devotee of Roman antiquities; in 1738–39, just after the death of his father, he returned to Italy. From this visit can be dated a huge influx of art that really determined the character of Castle Howard for the next century.

The 4th Earl's family life was not without tragedy: his first wife died in 1742 and within the space of five years he lost three sons and a daughter. With no

male heir the family line was in danger of dying out. His second wife, nearly half his age, was Isabella, daughter of Lord Byron of Newstead Abbey, Nottinghamshire. Their marriage lasted 15 years, during which time Isabella gave birth to a son, Frederick, who was only ten when he became the 5th Earl. He too enjoyed the cultural attractions of the Grand Tour, travelling to Italy in 1767–68. In 1770 he married Margaret Caroline Leveson Gower and the couple had ten children. Later, in April 1778, he was dispatched to North America as chief of the commissioners sent to talk with the colonists, but the mission was a failure. During his trip he penned a series of heartfelt letters to his wife, in which he reported terrific storms while at sea.

His extravagant lifestyle and his rash generosity in standing surety for the gambling debts of his close friend and fellow politician Charles James Fox nearly bankrupted the family. Gradually he repaired his finances and was able to oversee the completion of the house as well as continue his passion for collecting, and late in his life he turned his attention to farming. Frederick's son George became 6th Earl of Carlisle in 1825. His marriage in 1801 to Georgiana Cavendish, the eldest daughter of the famous Georgiana, 5th Duchess of Devonshire,

ABOVE LEFT George Howard, 6th Earl of Carlisle, by Sir Thomas Lawrence, c.1825.

ABOVE RIGHT Georgiana, 6th Countess of Carlisle, by Robert Thorburn, 1853.

united the great Whig houses of Castle Howard and Chatsworth. Between 1802 and 1823 she gave birth to 12 children who married into other aristocratic families. Little wonder that the Tory Prime Minister Sir Robert Peel is supposed to have exclaimed in the 1830s, 'Damn the Whigs, they are all cousins'.

Georgiana was exceptionally close to her eldest son, George, the bachelor 7th Earl. As a young man he maintained the family tradition of Continental travel, visiting France and Italy in 1823. During the 1830s he was appointed Chief Secretary to Ireland, but when he lost his parliamentary seat in 1840 he spent a year travelling through North America, where he was greatly impressed with the scenery. His favourite sight was Niagara Falls, which he described as God's 'sublimest temple'.

RIGHT George Howard, 7th Earl of Carlisle, by Ernst Wilhelm Rietschel, 1854.

Deeply opposed to slavery, the 7th Earl was shocked to witness enslaved people at work on plantations. In 1852 the author Harriet Beecher Stowe asked him to write the preface to the English edition of her novel *Uncle Tom's Cabin*. The earl admired the book greatly, which was a publishing phenomenon on both sides of the Atlantic.

He was succeeded by another bachelor, his brother William, during whose illness the estate was administered by trustees until his nephew George Howard became 9th Earl of Carlisle in 1889. In 1863 the young George had met Rosalind Stanley, who came from a political family, and a year later the couple married. Over the course of 19 years Rosalind gave birth to five daughters and six sons. Aware that her husband's passion in life was his art, she asked to be allowed to manage the family estates, totalling 78,000 acres.

The 9th Earl died in 1911 and Rosalind in 1921, by which time the family estates had been divided among their surviving children. Their eldest son Charles became 10th Earl and chose to live at Naworth Castle, which meant that the family title left Castle Howard. His younger brother Geoffrey lived at Castle Howard and maintained the family tradition of sitting in Parliament

ABOVE LEFT George Howard, 9th Earl of Carlisle, by George Frederic Watts, 1865–67.

ABOVE RIGHT Rosalind, 9th Countess of Carlisle, by Frederic, Lord Leighton, 1865–67.

ABOVE LEFT Geoffrey
William Algernon Howard
by George Sephton, 1895.

ABOVE RIGHT Ethel 'Kitty'
Methuen by Emil Otto
Hoppé, c.1910.

as a Liberal MP, serving as an aide to Prime Minister Herbert Asquith. In 1915 he married Ethel 'Kitty' Methuen and they had five children, Christian, Mark, George, Christopher and Katherine. The couple died in the 1930s before their children came of age, and at this point the family trustees suggested it might be a good time to dispose of Castle Howard: the common feeling was that such grand houses were white elephants, too expensive to staff and maintain. But these deliberations were halted by the outbreak of war in September 1939.

What followed were the darkest days for the family. In November 1940, while the house was occupied by a girls' school, fire ravaged the building, destroying 20 rooms and the great dome. The three sons were away on service: Mark died in Normandy in 1944, and in the same year the youngest son Christopher died while flying with the RAF in 617 Dambusters Squadron; the middle son George was far away in Burma, where he was wounded in action. By the end of the war he found himself the inheritor of Castle Howard and returned to a severely damaged building, with the grounds overgrown, the woods felled and the splendid array of eighteenth-century monuments in danger of collapse.

ABOVE LEFT George Anthony Geoffrey Howard by Trevor Stubley, 1981.

ABOVE RIGHT Simon Howard, c.2010.

LEFT Lady Cecilia Howard, c.1955.

RIGHT Nicholas Howard, 2025.

FAR RIGHT Victoria Howard, 2025.

At the end of the decade George made the momentous decision to keep Castle Howard as a family home. The school vacated the building, and after his marriage in 1949 to Lady Cecilia Fitzroy the couple moved into the house, where they brought up their four sons. Then, in 1952, he was among a handful of stately-home owners who opened their doors to the public. He also began restoring the house and estate. Not only did he revive Castle Howard's fortunes but also its popularity, especially when he offered the house as a location for the world-famous filming of *Brideshead Revisited*, first broadcast in 1981.

In later years he divided his time between running Castle Howard and public life. In 1982 he was appointed Chairman of the Governors of the BBC and he was made a life peer in 1983, taking the title of Lord Howard of Henderskelfe. Following George Howard's death, Castle Howard was run first by his son Simon, who stepped down in 2015 when his brother Nicholas and wife Victoria took over the estate.

Family Tree

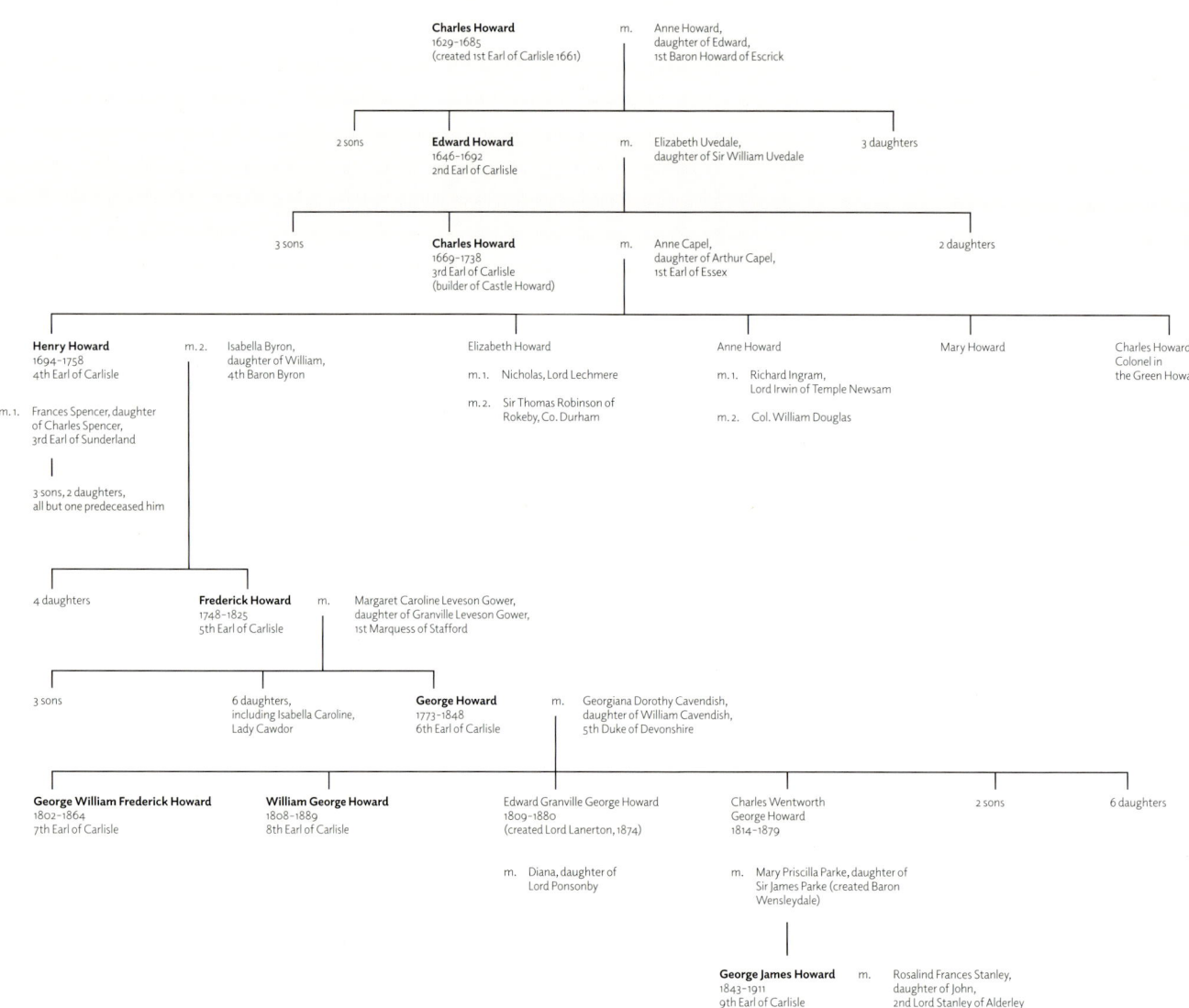

Charles Howard
1629–1685
(created 1st Earl of Carlisle 1661)

m. Anne Howard,
daughter of Edward,
1st Baron Howard of Escrick

2 sons

Edward Howard
1646–1692
2nd Earl of Carlisle

m. Elizabeth Uvedale,
daughter of Sir William Uvedale

3 daughters

3 sons

Charles Howard
1669–1738
3rd Earl of Carlisle
(builder of Castle Howard)

m. Anne Capel,
daughter of Arthur Capel,
1st Earl of Essex

2 daughters

Henry Howard
1694–1758
4th Earl of Carlisle

m. 2. Isabella Byron,
daughter of William,
4th Baron Byron

Elizabeth Howard

m. 1. Nicholas, Lord Lechmere

m. 2. Sir Thomas Robinson of
Rokeby, Co. Durham

Anne Howard

m. 1. Richard Ingram,
Lord Irwin of Temple Newsam

m. 2. Col. William Douglas

Mary Howard

Charles Howard,
Colonel in
the Green Howards

m. 1. Frances Spencer, daughter
of Charles Spencer,
3rd Earl of Sunderland

3 sons, 2 daughters,
all but one predeceased him

4 daughters

Frederick Howard
1748–1825
5th Earl of Carlisle

m. Margaret Caroline Leveson Gower,
daughter of Granville Leveson Gower,
1st Marquess of Stafford

3 sons

6 daughters,
including Isabella Caroline,
Lady Cawdor

George Howard
1773–1848
6th Earl of Carlisle

m. Georgiana Dorothy Cavendish,
daughter of William Cavendish,
5th Duke of Devonshire

George William Frederick Howard
1802–1864
7th Earl of Carlisle

William George Howard
1808–1889
8th Earl of Carlisle

Edward Granville George Howard
1809–1880
(created Lord Lanerton, 1874)

Charles Wentworth
George Howard
1814–1879

2 sons

6 daughters

m. Diana, daughter of
Lord Ponsonby

m. Mary Priscilla Parke, daughter of
Sir James Parke (created Baron
Wensleydale)

George James Howard
1843–1911
9th Earl of Carlisle

m. Rosalind Frances Stanley,
daughter of John,
2nd Lord Stanley of Alderley

Continued opposite

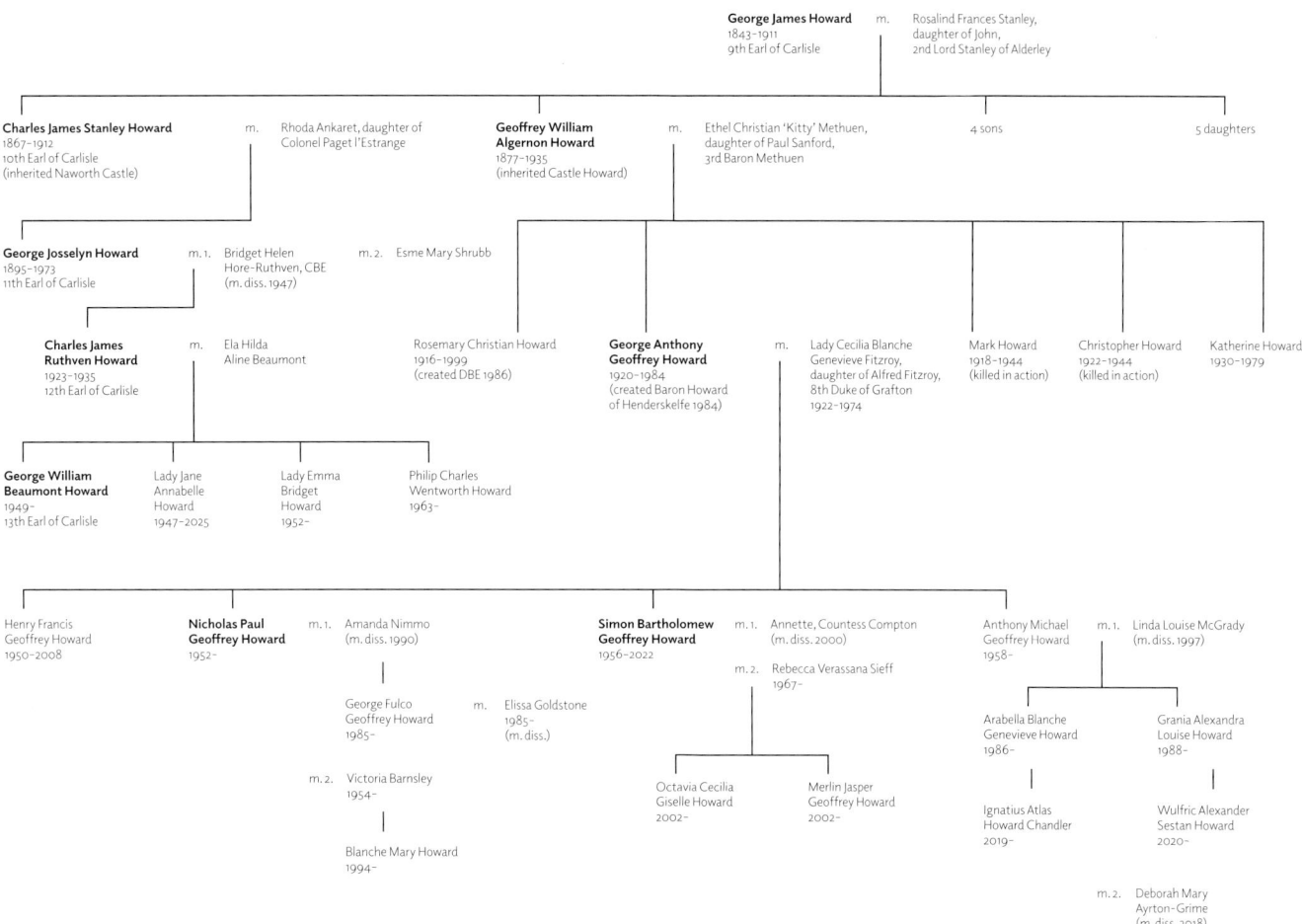

George James Howard
1843-1911
9th Earl of Carlisle
m. Rosalind Frances Stanley,
daughter of John,
2nd Lord Stanley of Alderley

Charles James Stanley Howard
1867-1912
10th Earl of Carlisle
(inherited Naworth Castle)
m. Rhoda Ankaret, daughter of
Colonel Paget l'Estrange

Geoffrey William
Algernon Howard
1877-1935
(inherited Castle Howard)
m. Ethel Christian 'Kitty' Methuen,
daughter of Paul Sanford,
3rd Baron Methuen

4 sons

5 daughters

George Josselyn Howard
1895-1973
11th Earl of Carlisle
m.1. Bridget Helen
Hore-Ruthven, CBE
(m. diss. 1947)
m.2. Esme Mary Shrubb

Charles James
Ruthven Howard
1923-1935
12th Earl of Carlisle
m. Ela Hilda
Aline Beaumont

Rosemary Christian Howard
1916-1999
(created DBE 1986)

George Anthony
Geoffrey Howard
1920-1984
(created Baron Howard
of Henderskelfe 1984)
m. Lady Cecilia Blanche
Genevieve Fitzroy,
daughter of Alfred Fitzroy,
8th Duke of Grafton
1922-1974

Mark Howard
1918-1944
(killed in action)

Christopher Howard
1922-1944
(killed in action)

Katherine Howard
1930-1979

George William
Beaumont Howard
1949-
13th Earl of Carlisle

Lady Jane
Annabelle
Howard
1947-2025

Lady Emma
Bridget
Howard
1952-

Philip Charles
Wentworth Howard
1963-

Henry Francis
Geoffrey Howard
1950-2008

Nicholas Paul
Geoffrey Howard
1952-
m.1. Amanda Nimmo
(m. diss. 1990)

Simon Bartholomew
Geoffrey Howard
1956-2022
m.1. Annette, Countess Compton
(m. diss. 2000)
m.2. Rebecca Verassana Sieff
1967-

Anthony Michael
Geoffrey Howard
1958-
m.1. Linda Louise McGrady
(m. diss. 1997)

George Fulco
Geoffrey Howard
1985-
m. Elissa Goldstone
1985-
(m. diss.)

m.2. Victoria Barnsley
1954-

Blanche Mary Howard
1994-

Octavia Cecilia
Giselle Howard
2002-

Merlin Jasper
Geoffrey Howard
2002-

Arabella Blanche
Genevieve Howard
1986-

Grania Alexandra
Louise Howard
1988-

Ignatius Atlas
Howard Chandler
2019-

Wulfric Alexander
Sestan Howard
2020-

m.2. Deborah Mary
Ayrton-Grime
(m. diss. 2018)

The Men Who Made Castle Howard

Castle Howard owes its creation to three people, the 3rd Earl as patron and his two talented architects: Sir John Vanbrugh and the immensely experienced Nicholas Hawksmoor, who had worked closely with Sir Christopher Wren for many years. They were assisted by a host of English and Continental craftsmen and artists such as Antonio Pellegrini and Henri Nadauld. In turn, Sir Thomas Robinson, who married into the family, began the west wing in the 1750s, although the interiors were finally decorated by Charles Heathcote Tatham. During the 1780s John Carr of York built the stables. At the end of the nineteenth century two more visionaries placed their stamp on the building: William Morris and Edward Burne-Jones, who designed the chapel with its stained-glass windows. Outdoors, the eighteenth-century landscape of Vanbrugh and Hawksmoor was modified by William Andrews Nesfield in the 1850s. In the twentieth century plantsman James Russell replanted Ray Wood and developed the Arboretum; indoors, family

OPPOSITE LEFT Sir John Vanbrugh by Sir Godfrey Kneller, c.1705. Vanbrugh was a colourful character who had been a trader in India with the East India Company, a marine and prisoner of the French, and a successful London playwright before turning to architecture.

OPPOSITE RIGHT Nicholas Hawksmoor, after a bust attributed to Sir Henry Cheere, 1736.

ABOVE LEFT John Carr by Sir William Beechey, after 1790.

ABOVE RIGHT Sir Thomas Robinson by Frans van der Mijn, 1750.

friend Felix Kelly painted the murals for the restored Garden Hall and the young architect Julian Bicknell designed the New Library in 1980. Each generation of the family worked closely with many different designers, craftsmen, architects and artists. But these figures have one thing in common: they all shared the vision for Castle Howard.

The Women of Castle Howard

Traditionally Castle Howard has been defined in terms of the male figures, but wives, mothers, sisters and daughters have also shaped the house and family, as recorded in the archives.

Mary, Anne and Elizabeth, the three daughters of the 3rd Earl, were painted by Pellegrini in c.1709–12. The portrait depicts them as identical, each an eligible heiress, but their copious correspondence with their father reveals three distinct individuals: Mary, who suffered from hypochondria and remained single; Anne, who was an author and traveller and was twice widowed; and Elizabeth, who enjoyed gambling and married Sir Thomas Robinson.

Isabella, the 4th Countess, their sister-in-law, was an energetic chatelaine in the 1750s, redecorating rooms and managing domestic expenditure. She compiled a 'Book of Receipts' containing around 200 culinary recipes, medicinal remedies and household tips. Her other skills included etching, botany and upholstery, and she found fame as the author of an advice manual for young ladies.

In 1814 Caroline, Lady Cawdor, the 5th Earl's daughter, toured Europe with her husband and left a colourful account of her journeys. Travelling with her *necessaire* (a portable tea service), she would make tea whenever she arrived at new lodgings. In Italy she climbed Vesuvius; then, returning through Paris, she learnt that her brother Frederick had just been killed at the Battle of Waterloo.

Georgiana, the 6th Countess, was a devoted mother to her children and, despite suffering from melancholy for much of her life, she supervised the household closely and was responsible for a fresh wave of improvements in the 1840s. No detail escaped her attention: she warned against the smells of fresh paint; ordered double glazing for the winter months; became irate when trees were felled without her knowledge; and in 1850 welcomed Queen Victoria and Prince Albert to Castle Howard.

At the end of the nineteenth century Rosalind, the 9th Countess, took on the management of the family estates, supervising farming, forestry, the welfare of tenants, local

LEFT The Three Daughters of the 3rd Earl of Carlisle by Antonio Pellegrini, c.1709–12.

education and temperance. Her great crusade was women's suffrage and she became President of the Women's Liberal Federation. She believed in constitutional change and disagreed with the direct-action tactics of the Suffragettes, dismissing them as 'impatient, lawless, scolding women, with hate in their hearts'.

In the aftermath of the fire of 1940 Rosalind's granddaughter Christian moved into the gatehouse and kept a watchful eye on Castle Howard. A keen advocate for the ordination of women in the Church of England, she was made a dame in 1999. After the Second World War Lady Cecilia Howard, with her husband George, worked hard to turn Castle Howard back from a school to a family home and a visitor attraction. She helped dress and arrange the rooms, and in the early days handed out tickets at the entrance. Victoria Howard OBE founded the publishing house 4th Estate and subsequently was CEO of HarperCollins for 13 years. In 2015 she came to run Castle Howard with her husband Nicholas, steering the business through the Covid pandemic and masterminding the rejuvenation of the house and estate.

ABOVE FROM LEFT
Isabella, 4th Countess of Carlisle, by Michael Dahl, c.1735-40; Isabella Caroline, Lady Cawdor, by Henry Bone, 1800; Georgiana, 6th Countess of Carlisle, by John Jackson c.1808.

BELOW Rosalind, 9th Countess of Carlisle, by Dante Gabriel Rossetti, 1870.

THE HOUSE

Timeline

1600s

1689 Accession of William and Mary; the Bill of Rights.

1696 Premier of *The Relapse*, Vanbrugh's first play at Drury Lane

1698 The 3rd Earl takes a lease on the lands and castle of Henderskelfe from his grandmother.

1699 Designs for Castle Howard evolve and by the end of the year foundations begin to be dug.

1700s

1701 Work progresses on the east wing and garden front.

1706 Built from east to west, the house assumes its shape as the central block is completed.

1715 House is complete save for the west wing; work moves to the gardens and grounds.

1720 South Sea Bubble, the first major stock market crash.

1726 Vanbrugh dies with the Temple of the Four Winds unfinished.

1738 3rd Earl dies with the mausoleum incomplete.

1742 First performance of George Frideric Handel's oratorio *Messiah*.

1758 Robinson's west wing is built, but the interior is not finished for another 50 years.

1776 American Declaration of Independence.

1782 Stables built by John Carr of York.

1797 Great Lake completed and flooded.

1800s

1801 Act of Union between Great Britain and Ireland.

1811 Long Gallery completed.

1825 Opening of Stockton-Darlington railway.

1838 Charles Dickens publishes *Oliver Twist*.

1841 The 7th Earl travels to North America.

1850 Nesfield installs the fountains and parterre, and Queen Victoria visits.

1851 The Great Exhibition.

1870 Chapel refurbished by Morris & Co. The 7th Earl's monument is completed.

1890 Nesfield's parterre is partially dismantled.

1895 National Trust is founded.

1900S

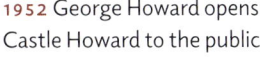

1911 Family estates divided among the 9th Earl's children.

1914 Outbreak of the First World War.

1940 Queen Margaret's School for Girls occupies the house and fire breaks out in the south-east wing.

1952 George Howard opens Castle Howard to the public.

1960 Vanbrugh's dome is rebuilt, and is redecorated by Scott Medd.

1967 The Beatles release the album *Sgt. Pepper's Lonely Hearts Club Band*.

1981 *Brideshead Revisited* is broadcast on British television.

1989 The World Wide Web is invented by Tim Berners-Lee.

1993 Central block of the house is re-roofed.

2000S

2009 Barack Obama becomes the first African American President of the USA.

2014 Parts of the lime Avenue are replanted.

2019 Skelf Island children's adventure playground is opened.

2020 Worldwide Covid pandemic.

2024 Castle Howard Foundation is established.

2025 Castle Howard's '21st Century Renaissance' is launched.

Building History:
Eighteenth to Twentieth Centuries

In the late seventeenth century many aristocrats in England were busy either improving their houses or commissioning new mansions. Among them was the 3rd Earl of Carlisle who approached William Talman, the leading country house architect of the day, to furnish him with designs for a new house. However, he rejected Talman's proposals, and in the summer of 1699 turned to his fellow Kit-Cat Club member, the dramatist Vanbrugh, who, at that point, had never built anything in his life.

How Vanbrugh, with no architectural experience, was able to convince Carlisle that he was the right choice remains a mystery: the bravado of the amateur, the experienced man of the theatre, someone who was keen to try his hand at anything, the genial camaraderie of the Kit-Cat Club, as well as his immense charm – all of these must have contributed to their fruitful relationship.

Between 1699 and 1702 the design for the house evolved. Two projecting wings always featured in the proposals, but the notion of a huge crowning

BELOW Early sketch proposal for Castle Howard by Vanbrugh, c.1699–1706.

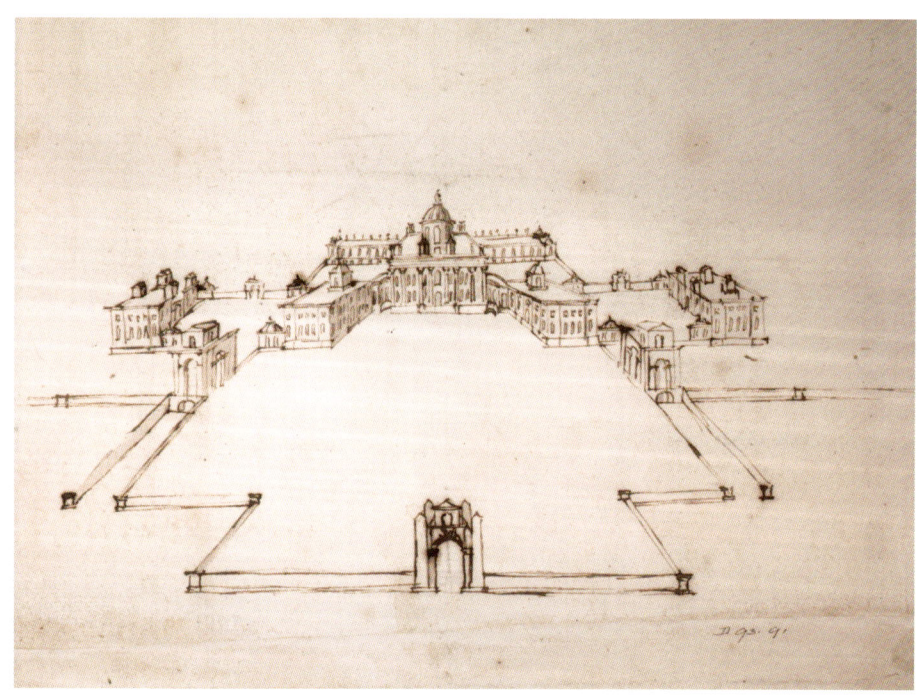

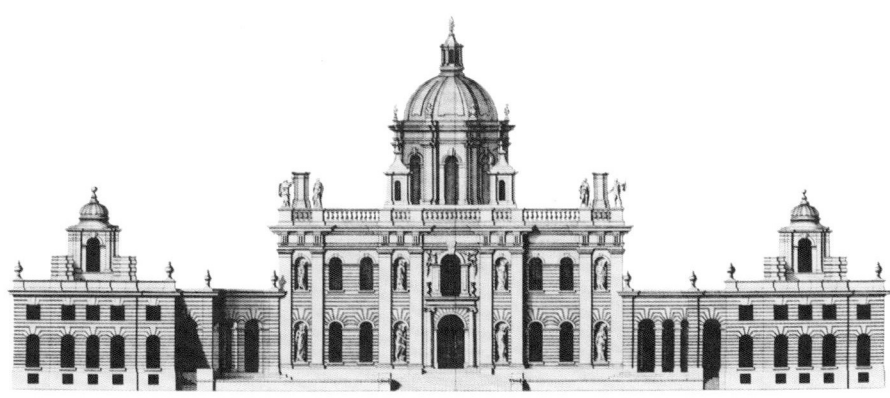

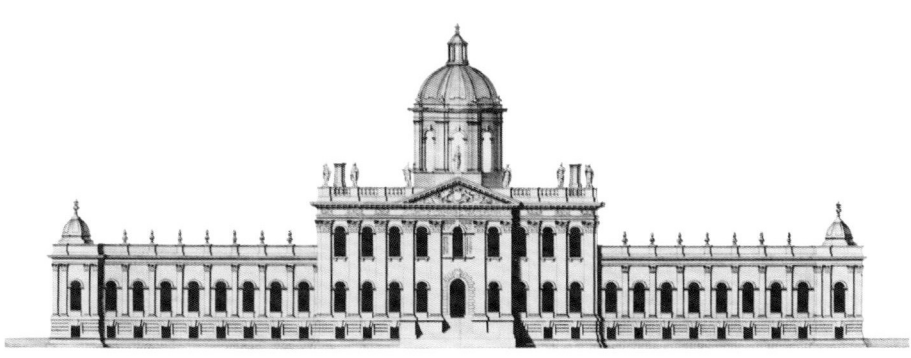

ABOVE The north and south elevations of Castle Howard from Volume 1 of *Vitruvius Britannicus* (1715).

dome came a little later. Vanbrugh, who had recruited the seasoned architect Hawksmoor to assist him, orientated the building on a north–south axis, which enabled the south-facing apartments to be brightly illuminated in daylight.

Castle Howard was capped with a huge masonry lantern and dome, the first to crown a private residence in England. The façades were filled with carved decoration, including coronets, ciphers and a coat of arms. Statues and urns filled the niches and the skyline presented a vast dramatic spectacle. There were different orders for the pilasters of the two fronts: Doric for the north, Corinthian for the south. When challenged over this, Hawksmoor retorted that nobody could see both fronts simultaneously. In 1715 elevations of both fronts appeared in a major architectural publication of the day, *Vitruvius Britannicus*.

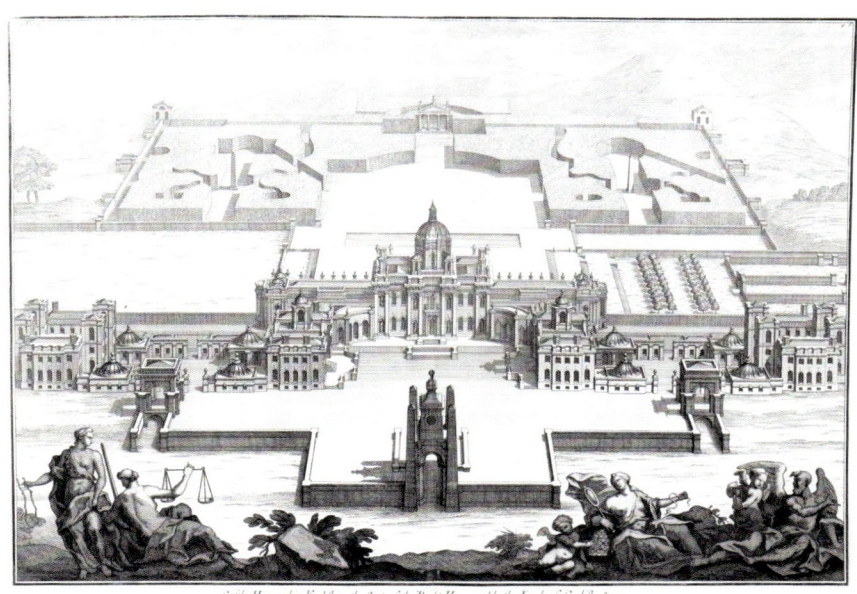

LEFT The bird's-eye view of Castle Howard from Volume 3 of *Vitruvius Britannicus* (1725). At this time one visitor commented, 'there will be found few houses in England of such splendour and so large dimensions'.

BELOW A contemporary bird's-eye view of the house; the mismatching wings are immediately apparent both in size and style.

Carlisle's building project became the talk of fashionable society and by 1725, when a new engraving of the house appeared in the third volume of *Vitruvius Britannicus*, much of the exterior structure was complete and its interiors opulently finished. This striking view revealed to the world at large the full magnificence of the buildings and grounds, which during some years had cost Carlisle nearly a third of his annual income.

But the bird's-eye view represents a building that was far from finished, and never completed in the manner shown. The house lacked a matching west wing and was to do so for another quarter of a century. One of the reasons for this was that from roughly 1715 onwards Carlisle had diverted much of his energy and income into landscaping the surrounding terrain.

Vanbrugh was anxious that the house should receive its symmetrical west wing, but when he died in 1726 the house was still incomplete. It remained so when the 3rd Earl died in 1738. It was another two decades before the building began to be finished by Carlisle's son-in-law, the amateur architect Robinson. In the 1750s he began the west wing, which he designed in the Palladian style that had eclipsed the earlier Baroque taste. Inspired in part by William Kent's designs for the Houses of Parliament, Robinson designed a broad wing with a lengthy western façade. It has a low rustic storey and a *piano nobile* above, with a central octagonal dome and attic pavilions at each end with pyramid roofs.

The Chimney Side of the Gallery as finished.

When the 4th Earl died in 1758 the west wing was only partially finished and lacked a roof and first floor. Things were a little more advanced at the time of Robinson's death in 1777, with the roof completed but the interiors unfinished, as the trustees of the young 5th Earl had refused to spend more money on the work.

From the outside the unbalanced appearance of the house provoked a mixed response from viewers, many of whom were dissatisfied with the lack of symmetry. One visitor in 1778 imagined the two distinct wings to 'stand staring at each other, as much as to say, *What business have you here?*'. In his reminiscences the 5th Earl remembered how the family found it difficult to comprehend their father's decision to allow a new wing 'not correspondent to the other, or to the centre part of the house'. The construction of Castle Howard was finally completed with Tatham's decoration of the Long Gallery between 1801 and 1811, more than a century after building had begun, spanning the lifetimes of three earls and numerous architects and craftsmen.

Today, therefore, the house bears only a partial resemblance to the idealised view in *Vitruvius Britannicus*, with its two identical wings: instead, the wings do not match, with Vanbrugh's Baroque sitting cheek-by-jowl with Robinson's Palladian addition. It would be a mistake to dismiss Robinson's wing as inferior, however. The western elevation is grand in its own right and the interiors every bit as convenient and magnificent as Robinson boasted they would be. This protracted building history means that Castle Howard is an intriguing mix of architectural styles.

One building that was finished in the second half of the eighteenth century was a new stable block to the west of the house. This was built to the designs of John Carr between 1781 and 1784. On the north side is a triumphal archway flanked by four giant columns. With the rise of the motor car the stables gradually became redundant, but when Castle Howard opened in 1952 the block was converted, first into a series of costume galleries before becoming the entrance complex for visitors.

Although Castle Howard is celebrated as an extraordinary Baroque house, it has experienced change and modification repeatedly. There have been constant cycles of redecoration taking advantage of new fashions, and alterations indoors and outdoors. Nevertheless, the house today would be largely recognisable to its eighteenth-century creators. Apart from Robinson's work and the construction of the chapel a century later, the building never underwent any wholesale transformation at a later date. It was not ripped down and built in an entirely new style, nor was it given a full Victorian makeover. The most momentous instance of change came about by accident in the twentieth century.

During the Second World War Queen Margaret's School for Girls occupied Castle Howard. On the morning of 9 November 1940 calamity struck, when fire broke out in the south-east wing. It is believed the cause was a chimney fire or an electrical fault. Flames raged through the house into the Great Hall, destroying the dome and nearly 20 rooms. For the next few years much of Castle Howard was open to the skies, its once splendid rooms gutted shells. George Howard, who inherited Castle Howard after the war, was determined to recover Vanbrugh's architectural masterpiece. The traces of the school were stripped away, and the rooms refreshed and filled with furniture and pictures that had been in store throughout the war years, prior to opening to the public in 1952. It is due to the remarkable efforts of George Howard and his wife Lady Cecilia that Castle Howard is still a family home and enjoys such popularity with the public.

In 1960–62 the dome was rebuilt, returning the house to its original Vanbrugh glory. In 1981, in conjunction with Granada Television and the filming of *Brideshead Revisited*, the Garden Hall was reconstructed, and shortly afterwards the New Library. As time and money permit, the gradual task of restoring the fire-damaged sections has continued: in 1994–95 the central block was re-roofed and two bedrooms below restored; in 2021 the east wing lead roof was renewed at a cost of more than £1 million; and in 2025 the Tapestry Drawing Room was created from a burnt interior.

All over the house restoration and essential maintenance are ongoing, from larger projects dealing with masonry, lead roofing and the painting of the window frames (a five-year project), to upgrading electrics, heating and fire protection, to smaller work on conserving paintings, furniture and textiles.

This constant work testifies to the family's dedication to Castle Howard. Today nearly 300,000 visitors a year are welcomed in the house and grounds, including to the spectacular Christmas displays, while many more attend various functions and events.

Grand Staircase, China Landing and Antique Passage

The interior of Castle Howard was designed around simple principles: at the heart of the house is the Great Hall, from where the central block divides on the south side into private apartments created for the 3rd Earl and state apartments for a visiting monarch. To the north were two projecting wings with more domestic quarters and, in time, the Long Gallery and chapel. But what began life as a public palace changed as the 3rd Earl's political career came to an end; instead Castle Howard became a magnificent private residence.

Today the Grand Staircase, constructed in the 1870s, provides a majestic entrance to the west wing. Beneath the skylight, with its 74 panes of glass, hang plaster bas-reliefs of famous antique works. These complement the antique sculpture at the foot of the stairs and throughout the house.

BELOW LEFT The Grand Staircase.

BELOW RIGHT The marble altar said to be from the Temple of the Oracle at Delphi in Greece. This was given to the 5th Earl by Sir William Hamilton after Horatio Nelson had saved it from falling into French hands in Naples in 1798.

RIGHT The Victorian mahogany cabinet was moved to this location in 1882 and enlarged to 12 bays. It houses porcelain from the factories of Sèvres, Meissen, Chelsea and Derby.

The staircase is the first hint of a dramatic architectural sequence of marble floors and long, stone-walled corridors that lead through the Antique Passage to the climax of the painted Great Hall with its flanking staircases and dome.

At the top of the Grand Staircase is the China Landing, ornamented with a classical cornice and frieze decorated with bucrania (ox skulls). Vanbrugh's original design had always featured two immense parallel passages running the length of the house from east to west, providing a spectacular vista. Contrary to all expectations, they were not draughty. In the winter of 1713 Vanbrugh proudly recorded 'Though we have now had as bitter storms as rain and wind

LEFT The Antique Passage. The numerous parcel-gilt wooden pedestals and tables date from the 1740s and were commissioned by the 4th Earl directly on his return from Italy. The marble columns and stone pedestals that support some of the other sculptures were also acquired at the same time. Today the antiquities belong to the National Museums Liverpool as part of an in-lieu tax settlement, but because they are so integral to the identity of the house they remain *in situ* at Castle Howard.

BELOW LEFT One of a pair of marble sculptures depicting a lion attacking a bull, purchased by the 4th Earl.

BELOW RIGHT Plaster bust of Antinous, c.1700.

can compose, every room in the House is like an oven, and in the corridors 200 feet long there is not air enough in motion to stir the flame of a candle'.

The first detailed listing of the 4th Earl's treasures is dated 1759, one year after his death. By this time visitors were astonished at the quantities of sculpture on view: the larger statues were located in the Great Hall, and the completion of the west wing and Antique Passage in the early nineteenth century enabled this enormous collection to be displayed more expansively.

Both sections of the Antique Passage are lined with busts, statues, marble tabletops and urns, collected chiefly by the 4th Earl during his second visit to Italy in 1738–39. The majority of these pieces date from the first or second century AD, although, some like the colossal bust in plaster of Antinous, are eighteenth-century copies.

The 4th Earl was a discriminating collector and connoisseur of antiquities. His correspondence with the agents he employed in Italy to seek out sculptures, urns, bronzes and gems reveals him arguing over the price and quality of his purchases. These letters are a fascinating insight into the practicalities of collecting while on the Grand Tour: we read of the rivalry between the earl's agents, the shipping arrangements, anxieties about pirates intercepting vessels and the fear of storms and shipwreck. By the early 1740s these treasures began to reach Yorkshire safely.

The Grand Tour

The eighteenth-century Grand Tour was seen as a mixture of education and pleasure. Young men (and most Tourists were male) would travel overland through France (providing the English and French were not at war) before crossing the Alps and travelling down the Italian peninsula. The principal destinations were usually Rome, Florence and Venice, and later in the century Naples. Generally Rome and Florence were perceived as serious places for study, and the pursuit of such masculine activities as antiquarianism and connoisseurship. By contrast, Venice, 'La Serenissima' as she was proclaimed, was a more feminine destination. It was a place of ease and gratification, with masked balls and public pageants often featuring the Doge and officials of the Republic in flotillas on the lagoon and the Grand Canal.

For some aristocrats pleasure prevailed at the expense of education; others dutifully and enthusiastically absorbed the art and culture of ancient and contemporary Rome and rarely returned home empty-handed. Following in their footsteps would be ships and carriages transporting treasures they had purchased on these expeditions, which were destined for their magnificent houses in England. Six consecutive generations of Howards travelled to Italy, as well as further afield to Russia, Greece, Turkey, Africa, India and North America, so it is no surprise the house is filled with objects collected on their tours. Castle Howard is a Grand Tour house par excellence.

LEFT An eighteenth-century watercolour view of the Pantheon, very likely by an Italian artist and aimed at the tourist market.

ABOVE *The Bucintoro Preparing to Leave the Molo on Ascension Day* by Bernardo Bellotto, c.1739.

RIGHT A tiny watercolour view of Mount Vesuvius across the Bay of Naples, taken from an album compiled by Georgiana, 5th Duchess of Devonshire, in the 1790s.

Great Hall

The Great Hall is the crowning masterpiece of Vanbrugh's design. From the outside the dome presents Castle Howard with a unique silhouette, owing its inspiration to Wren's dome at St Paul's Cathedral, which Vanbrugh and Hawksmoor knew well. Inside, the hall rises 21 metres high in a triumph of theatre and space. The corner piers support the superstructure; two large arches open to reveal the walls and staircases on either side; a balcony traverses the upper level; and above are the tall stone lantern and gallery, with light flooding in from eight windows.

The painted decoration, executed by the Venetian artist Pellegrini between 1709 and 1712, depicts the *Four Elements* in the pendentives, the *Twelve Figures of the Zodiac* on the ceilings and *Apollo and the Muses* on the staircase wall. This ethereal world climaxes with the tale of Phaeton falling from his father's chariot on the underside of the cupola. Encouraged to look higher and higher, the viewer finally meets the dizzying spectacle of Apollo's son plunging to earth. The 3rd Earl and Vanbrugh revelled in the playful ironies of this dramatic tale of ambition and fall, which sits on top of the most ambitious house in England in its day.

The composite capitals in the corners with their massive acanthus leaves were carved by the Yorkshire mason Samuel Carpenter in 1705 and cost £84. The remainder of the stonework was carved by the Huguenot sculptor

OPPOSITE The Great Hall is a tour de force of geometry and pattern with the straight lines of the fluted pilasters flowing into the curved arches. The hall can be appreciated from ground level, from halfway up the staircase, from the balcony and also from the upper gallery: each vantage point prompts the viewer to gaze upwards, downwards or across the expansive space.

BELOW The wrought-iron railings for the balcony, staircase and gallery are by the Derbyshire craftsman John Gardom, who worked at Castle Howard between 1705 and 1710.

Henri Nadauld, who was also responsible for much of the exterior decoration. Nadauld and his fellow craftsmen Gideon du Chesne, the Hervé brothers and John Gardom all worked at Chatsworth, Boughton and other houses in early eighteenth-century England. Their names frequently appear in country house account books as they moved from one commission to the next. Generally local craftsmen would be employed for the day-to-day work, with more specialist artists commissioned for the embellishment and ornamentation.

ABOVE There is a perfect architectural symmetry to the top of the hall, a circle within an arched square complemented by sculptural detail and painted scenes.

BELOW On the west side of the hall, the scagliola recess with Doric pilasters houses a statue of Bacchus that dates from the second century AD.

OVERLEAF The fireplace surround with the picture over the hearth of the Roman god Vulcan asleep in his forge, painted by Pellegrini in 1709-12.

The fireplace surround and the Bacchus niche were decorated by the Italian stuccoists Giovanni Bagutti and his assistant Signor Plura in 1711-12. They are among the earliest known examples in England of the revival of the Roman technique of scagliola: a mixture of plaster and marble fragments. The fireplace is decorated with the family cipher, a pair of reversed Cs, made from brass. The flue bends to the right and rises up through the stonework. There are more than 60 chimney pots on the roof at Castle Howard.

The High South

The floor above the Great Hall is reached by either of the two side staircases, from which dramatic views of the hall may be glimpsed through the magnificent arches that pierce the walls.

The suite of apartments on the first floor once comprised a painted saloon and two adjacent bedchambers. The High Saloon with its coved ceiling was spectacularly decorated in 1709-12 with murals by Pellegrini depicting scenes from the Trojan War. The bedrooms housed tall four-poster beds adorned with fine textile hangings. The rooms also offered a unique elevated view onto the South Parterre and wider landscape below. They were the most prestigious apartments in the house and were used to accommodate Queen Victoria and Prince Albert on their visit in 1850.

Sadly the entire floor was destroyed in the fire of 1940. Although a new lead roof for the central block was built in the 1990s, these southern interiors remain bare shells. Two bedrooms on the north side, however, have been fully restored. The space became a film set for the 2008 movie version of *Brideshead Revisited* and is now used for exhibitions.

OPPOSITE A rare view of the High Saloon before its destruction, showing scenes painted in 1709-12 by Pellegrini from Virgil's Roman epic *The Aeneid* telling the story of the fall of Troy. At the end of the nineteenth century Rosalind, the 9th Countess, covered the walls with Morris wallpaper, but in the 1920s her son Geoffrey removed the paper to expose the original decoration. Within two decades the entire room had been lost in the fire.

LEFT Stonework, ironwork, painted decoration and natural light from the dome above combine to transform the area into a theatrical experience. To the north, the sequence of receding arches centred upon the window even suggests the proscenium arch in a theatre – something very familiar to Vanbrugh from his experiences as a playwright.

Garden Hall and New Library

The Garden Hall leading off from the Great Hall marks the transition from the north to the south side of the building. Vanbrugh was keen for these suites of rooms to have a southern aspect and take advantage of natural light, as well as looking over the gardens.

To the east and west of the Garden Hall lie two grand apartments. The rooms are connected through their doorways, creating a grand vista or enfilade. The south front is about 90 metres long and it was once possible to stand at either end and look through a sequence of 11 doorways. The south-east wing remains a shell from the fire, but looking west from the Garden Hall one can still appreciate the view through five rooms.

The Garden Hall, like the High Saloon above, was decorated by Pellegrini and filled with overdoor paintings, mirrors and sculptures, most of which were lost in the fire that destroyed two-thirds of the south front. The filming of *Brideshead Revisited* by Granada Television in 1981 created an opportunity to begin the restoration of these rooms, first with a film set that was then turned

OPPOSITE The enfilade to the west through the state apartments. Before the fire this was matched by a similar vista to the east through the 3rd Earl's private apartments.

BELOW The Garden Hall. The series of *capriccios* painted by Felix Kelly in 1981 portray imaginary Vanbrugh buildings enveloped by lush vegetation. They have fictitious pedigrees and incorporate teasingly recognisable features from Vanbrugh's various houses. In the centre of the room is a plaster version of the Dying Gaul, acquired by the 5th Earl in Rome in 1768.

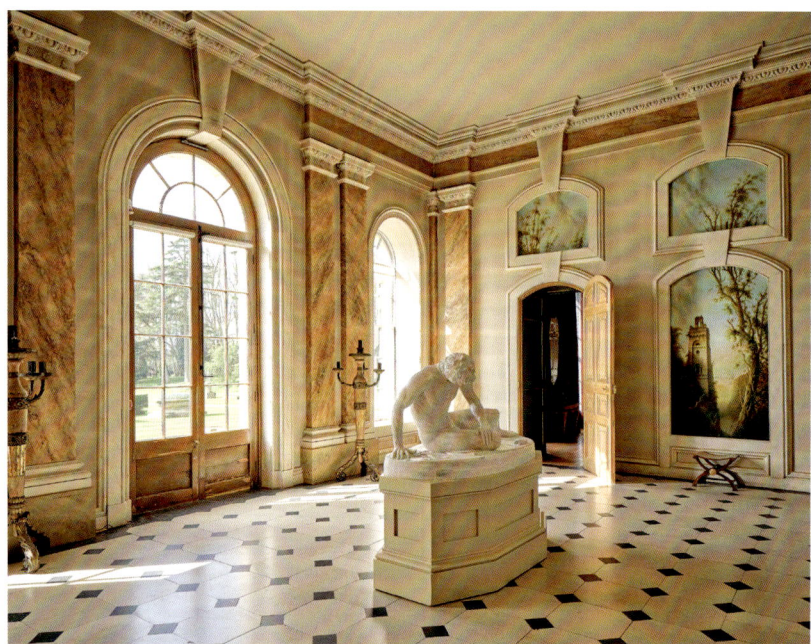

ABOVE AND LEFT
Two earlier views of the
Garden Hall: in the 1920s
before the fire, and in the
1950s after the fire. The
ceiling decoration, gilded
cornice with carved lions,
overdoor landscapes
by Marco Ricci, ornate
mirrors and the figure
of Venus by Sir Richard
Westmacott were all
destroyed. Only the base
of the column survived
the inferno.

BELOW The New Library
is filled with books on art,
architecture, natural
history, literature, music
and history, along with
private press books.

into a finished interior. No attempt was made to recreate the hall as before; instead George Howard, with his architect Julian Bicknell and the artist Felix Kelly, decided to rebuild in the spirit of Vanbrugh. The floor is of Portland stone and Welsh marble to match that of the Great Hall, and the doors are of oak from the estate.

To the east of the Garden Hall is the New Library, also designed by Bicknell in the shell that was once the Canaletto Room. As the collection of Venetian view paintings had mostly disappeared from Castle Howard, it was decided to create a wholly new room dedicated to housing parts of the vast library. Twenty-six bays were built, distinguished by their architectural form with pilasters and broken pediments on two walls. There is even a jib door that can swing shut enclosing occupants in an entirely book-lined space. The library is used by the family as an office and is open to the public at selected times of the year.

Tapestry Drawing Room

To the west of the Garden Hall is the first of the rooms in the state apartments designed by Vanbrugh. Originally completed in 1715 as a drawing room, it was fitted out with tapestries of the *Four Seasons* by John Vanderbank, after designs by the Dutch artist David Teniers. Dating from 1706, they were specially purchased from the Soho factory in London to hang in this room, and a letter from Hawksmoor explains how the light from the windows would illuminate them.

The room marked the westernmost point of the 1940 fire, and until recently the empty shell was used for temporary displays. The decision to reinstate the drawing room was driven by the opportunity to rehang the original tapestries in this space: they survived the fire because at the time

OPPOSITE A new frieze and fireplace surround made from plaster were designed by architect Francis Terry. The scene above is the Judgement of Paris by Marco Ricci. The picture left Castle Howard in 1991, but returned in 2025.

BELOW The recreation of the drawing room completes the enfilade that runs through the south-west wing.

they were in another part of the building. There are no original drawings of the room, but evidence in the archives and from similar period interiors elsewhere in England has guided the design of the panelling to fit the tapestries, the creation of a new cornice modelled on pre-fire photographs and the commissioning of a Baroque-style fireplace with plaster surround and overmantel picture inspired by the Great Hall.

While the room is not an exact recreation of its predecessor, it embodies the essence of an early eighteenth-century drawing room and has employed the traditional craft skills of joiners, plasterers, painters, upholsterers, gilders, furniture makers and conservators.

This mix of old and new includes not only the original tapestries, but also two suites of early eighteenth-century chairs. These were once covered in an eighteenth-century crimson damask, parts of which were from the original state bed hangings that were cut up and recycled at the end of the nineteenth century. Two double settees have been commissioned in the style of the eighteenth-century armchairs, reproducing every detail faithfully, and upholstered in cut velvet. The floor is covered with a late nineteenth-century Bessarabian kilim. Although this room has an unmistakably fresh feel, it has been designed to harmonise subtly with the other interiors in the house.

RIGHT On the east wall is a harbour view with men unloading fish on a quayside while merchants look on. In the background are battlements patrolled by guards.

Music Room

The Music Room was converted from a drawing room in the nineteenth century. The two Broadwood pianos, a small grand (1795) and a square piano (1805), both have five-and-a-half octave keyboards, unlike the eight octaves of modern times. The harp is also English, dating from c.1800. Making music was a regular pastime in the family, and the manuscript scores for the instruments are just a few from the large collection of compositions, sheet music and printed scores gathered in the eighteenth and nineteenth centuries.

The cornice, frieze, door surrounds and swags are of pinewood and carved by Daniel Hervé and Samuel Carpenter c.1705. On the eighteenth-century lacquer cabinet are blanc de chine figures of lions and kylins (Chinese mythical creatures). Dating from the Kangxi period (1661–1722), they are among the earliest pieces in the collection and exemplify the eighteenth-century European fashion for Chinese style.

The room contains many of the 5th Earl's Old Master paintings acquired during his Grand Tour, from London sale rooms and at the famous Orleans

OPPOSITE The Music Room with the Broadwood pianos.

BELOW The fireplace surround of Carrara marble decorated with vines, fruits and a ram's head is believed to date from c.1732. The two pairs of cassolettes on the mantelpiece, either side of the clock, are of Blue John and gilt bronze by the eighteenth-century inventor and engineer Matthew Boulton.

Collection sale in 1798. They include Annibale Carracci's *Portrait of a Gentleman*, thought to be a self-portrait; Girolamo Bedoli's *The Dukes of Ferrara*; Leandro Bassano's *Portrait of an Old Woman*, said to be his mother; Domenico Feti's *The Music Master*; Ferdinand Bol's *Portrait of an Old Man*; and Giovanni de Mio's *Allegory of the Arts and Sciences*.

Two Tudor portraits are a reminder of the origins of the family. Thomas Howard, 3rd Duke of Norfolk, from the studio of Hans Holbein c.1542, is depicted in his post as Earl Marshal of England and wearing a gold chain with the order of St George. Beside him is a portrait of his son Henry Howard, Earl of Surrey.

ABOVE Blanc de chine figures of Buddhist lions and kylins form a garniture on the top of the Chinese-style lacquer cabinet. The portrait of the bearded man (lower right) is by Ferdinand Bol.

RIGHT Henry Howard, Earl of Surrey, by George Sephton, 1909. This is a copy of a portrait by the Dutch artist William Scrots painted in 1546. Surrey is flamboyantly dressed and was one of the most painted noblemen in England – little wonder he attracted the envy of rival courtiers and the suspicions of Henry VIII. He was beheaded in December 1546.

Crimson Dining Room

In the eighteenth century this room was the state bedroom, but it later became a billiard room and was hung with tapestries. The present wall covering is a red silk damask introduced in the 1950s. The marble fireplace with a broken pediment is supported on Corinthian pillars, and the overmantel contains a sea view by Ricci.

The Kentian side tables date from c.1735, and the dining suite with parquetry triangular plate cupboards, side table and cellarette for holding wine bottles are George III in the style of Robert Adam. The room is still used for dining today and the table is laid with changing displays of silver and porcelain in settings for main or dessert courses. These might include Regency silver dishes by goldsmith Paul Storr (c.1810), a Crown Derby dessert service (1795) or a Meissen 'Red Dragon' service (c.1740).

OPPOSITE On the west wall of the Crimson Dining Room are landscapes by Gaspard Dughet and a harbour scene by Marco Ricci.

BELOW A Meissen 'Red Dragon' dinner service, c.1740, painted in brick red with dragons and flowers and comprising plates, tureens and bowls. The tureen handles are shaped in the form of lions' heads.

On the east wall are the three remaining Venetian view pictures in the collection, now recognised as by Bernardo Bellotto: *The Bucintoro Preparing to Leave the Molo on Ascension Day* and two less typical views with little or no water visible, including *The Campo San Stefano, Venice*. Hanging above is a picture of horses exercising on Newmarket Heath by John Wootton.

On the north wall are two landscape views of Castle Howard (c.1800) by Hendrik de Cort; *A Favourite Horse of Frederick, 5th Earl of Carlisle* (1773) by George Stubbs; *The 5th Earl of Carlisle with Members of his Family and Household in Phoenix Park, Dublin*, painted by Francis Wheatley in 1781 when the earl was Lieutenant of Ireland; and a *View of the Mall* (c.1710) in London by Marco Ricci – in the distance the London skyline features the newly built dome of St Paul's Cathedral.

ABOVE One of the mysteries of the room is the north doorway, with its frieze believed to be by Grinling Gibbons who is known to have received two payments in 1705–6. No convincing explanation has been found for its slanted angle.

RIGHT The cornice is decorated with brackets and flower heads beneath which is an ornate frieze depicting pairs of gilded lions among scrolling leafage. Both Samuel Carpenter and Daniel Hervé were responsible for much of the carving in this room.

BELOW RIGHT The head of a satyr from the first century AD stands in the broken pediment of the fireplace; below is a marble frieze of pigeons pecking at ears of corn. The fire surround beneath contains the family cipher of a pair of reversed Cs.

The Reynolds Room

In Vanbrugh's time this was the state dressing room in the apartments reserved for visiting royalty, but it was remodelled in the 1750s when Robinson constructed the west wing. It was enlarged into a three-bay drawing room and initially was hung with large tapestries of Roman scenes. By the 1770s it was earmarked by the 5th Earl to house his growing collection of paintings. After his purchases from the Orleans Collection sale in 1798 the room became a gallery of Old Master paintings, with pictures by Anthony van Dyck, Annibale Carracci, Orazio Gentileschi, Domenico Feti and Frans Snyders, among others.

In 1832 the amateur artist Mary Ellen Best visited Castle Howard and produced a watercolour view of the Orleans Room (as it was then named). The walls were densely filled with pictures. In the foreground is the housekeeper, Mrs Parker, who conducted visitors around the house; she is depicted holding a large bunch of keys.

This room has been redecorated and altered many times, but the house inventories in the archives make it possible to follow how it looked at different

BELOW Mary Ellen Best's painting records the 5th Earl's recent purchases of pictures, all of which are identifiable either at Castle Howard or in other collections. The Boulle clock in the corner and the figure of a boy riding a goat, seen through the doorway, can be found in the house today.

moments with fresh picture hangs and new arrangements of furniture. Most recently, in 2002, the walls were hung with a turquoise damask, which was also used to cover the suite of giltwood settees and chairs made by John Linnell in c.1775. It is still used as a drawing room, a space to which parties can withdraw after dinner.

The eighteenth-century serpentine Dutch cabinet contains a turquoise Meissen dinner service, c.1740, decorated with landscapes and harbour scenes. The porcelain figures are a mixture of Bow and Meissen, including a pair of colourful Malabar figures playing musical instruments that combine chinoiserie and Rococo styles.

The room is dominated by two large landscapes by Philip Roos, commonly known as Rosa di Tivoli, which were purchased in 1740. Alongside are pictures by Sir Joshua Reynolds, and in pride of place above the fireplace hangs the famous portrait of the 5th Earl in exactly the same position as shown in Best's

LEFT A French-style commode, inlaid with classical urns and festoons by the Swedish-born cabinet-maker Christopher Fuhrlohg, who signed and dated the piece 1767.

Frederick Howard,
5th Earl of Carlisle, by
Sir Joshua Reynolds, 1769.

watercolour. Painted in 1769, shortly after he had returned from his Grand Tour, the earl is wearing his robes as a Knight of the Thistle. His aristocratic hauteur is accentuated by the colours of his costume and the regalia he wears. He is captured descending steps with one hand pointing carelessly to his right; not for nothing is this known as an example of a 'swagger' portrait. But there is a more homely side to the picture. In the lower right corner Reynolds has depicted the earl's favourite dog, Rover, staring up at his master. During his travels through Europe the earl recorded Rover's many adventures: getting lost, fighting with other dogs, breaking a leg and peering enthusiastically over the precipices in the Alps. Alas, Rover did not return to England as he was run over by a carriage in Paris, leaving the earl heartbroken. The portrait is therefore a posthumous one of Rover. Reynolds was repeatedly commissioned to paint the family: in 1758 he had painted the earl as a young boy dressed in Van Dyck costume, and again in c.1770 with his friend George Selwyn. In the same year Reynolds began his portrait of Caroline, the 5th Countess, and in 1786 he produced a half-length of the earl's son George when he was Lord Morpeth.

GAINSBOROUGH AT CASTLE HOWARD

Girl with Pigs by Thomas Gainsborough, 1782. One of the artist's 'fancy' paintings, it dates from when Gainsborough had grown tired of painting society portraits and turned to his principal passion: landscapes and rural scenes. First exhibited in 1782, the picture was well received and Reynolds purchased it for 100 guineas. Gainsborough wrote to thank his fellow artist, wittily remarking, 'I may truly say I have brought my pigs to a fine market'. After Reynolds's death the painting was acquired by the 5th Earl in 1795, who commented favourably on the landscape and the young girl, although he had reservations about the pigs.

Museum Room

The Museum Room marks the boundary between Vanbrugh's Baroque south front and Robinson's Palladian west wing. Originally this corner room was known as the Grand Cabinet and was fitted with a tall west-facing bow window designed by Hawksmoor, but this was demolished by Robinson in the 1750s. He introduced different door surrounds, a deeper cornice and new windows, with a Venetian-style window on the south side. Hawksmoor's twin domes on the roof were replaced by a more classical attic storey with pyramid roof and upper windows, but this was lowered in the 1890s; only the cornice and gilded flowerhead frieze remains.

At this juncture in the building one can look back eastwards through the state rooms to the Garden Hall and also north into the Long Gallery next door. When Tatham came to complete the decoration in 1801–11 he envisaged

A CABINET FOR CURIOSITIES

The pair of Roman ebonised pietra dura cabinets date from the early seventeenth century and were acquired by the 4th Earl. Their drawers are inset with panels of lapis lazuli, agate and quartz, and the marble columns flanking a central compartment have gilt-bronze Corinthian capitals. These cabinets with drawers and cupboards would have been perfect for accommodating the earl's collection of small bronzes, coins, medals and intaglios. They rest on pier tables decorated with garlands of grapes and masks of Bacchus, with male and female figures serving as front legs.

the Museum Room as an antechamber to the Long Gallery, and it was filled with antiquities. The tables are c.1745, with mottled Peterhead granite tops on which rest two eighteenth-century busts made of Derbyshire fossil.

The embossed wallpaper was purchased by Rosalind, the 9th Countess, in 1886 from Maples & Co. in London at a cost of £41. It was designed in imitation of seventeenth-century Spanish leather wall hangings. The varied shadings reveal where the walls have been covered by paintings at different times.

Hanging alongside portraits of Charles II by Sir Peter Lely and of the Duke of Grafton by Willem Wissing are full-length portraits of the first four Earls of Carlisle. The 1st and 2nd Earls by Kneller were originally half-length, but when the 3rd Earl was painted by Aikman in 1728 he had these extended so that they were a matching set. This means that all three earls are wearing identical red-heeled shoes. The 4th Earl is likely to have commissioned the ornate matching frames by William Linnell after his portrait had been painted by Hudson in 1756.

ABOVE Tatham's engraving of 1811 shows how packed the room was with smaller antiquities. These were redisplayed throughout the house later in the century.

BELOW The ceiling and frieze were painted and gilded in 2024–25, giving the room a more Regency feel and clearly marking the division between the older Baroque part of the house and the later Palladian wing.

Long Gallery and Octagon

Finished in 1811 by Tatham, the Long Gallery was always intended as a neoclassical display space, as well as an interior large enough to hold assemblies and balls, such as when Queen Victoria and Prince Albert visited in 1850. The room divides into north and south sections with an Octagon in the centre: 33 lengths of the gallery equal one mile (1,609 metres).

Jackson's painting on the easel depicts the elderly 5th Earl with his son George shortly after the decoration was completed in c.1811. Some of the features in the picture are present today, including the George II tables with granite tops, Tatham's gilt-brass chandeliers and the marble busts by Joseph Nollekens of the 5th Earl (c.1768) and his friend and fellow politician Charles James Fox (1805).

RIGHT The 5th Earl of Carlisle and his son George in the Long Gallery by John Jackson, c.1811. There is a conceit in this picture: the painting on the easel that the two men are admiring is surely this very view of the gallery.

RIGHT The wine cooler made from bog oak and silver gilt was presented to Lord Morpeth, later the 7th Earl, as a consolation prize for his defeat in the general election of 1841. Costing more than one thousand guineas, it was decorated with plaques naming 26 towns in his West Riding constituency. Accompanying the cooler was a farewell petition signed by 50,000 of his constituents. When unrolled, it measures 120 metres in length.

OPPOSITE The Octagon lined with bookcases, portraits and a newly commissioned chandelier copied from the original ones by Tatham.

BELOW A *capriccio* view by Paolo Panini depicting the Colosseum, the Arch of Constantine and, in the foreground, the figure of the Dying Gaul. Inspired by this painting, the 5th Earl would purchase a full-size plaster version of the Gaul when he was in Rome in 1768.

Originally a stone colour, over the years the walls of the Long Gallery have been decorated in different styles, including with red 'Sunflower' pattern Morris wallpaper in the 1880s. The present scheme was completed in 2025 with a new picture hang by Alec Cobbe, a bespoke colour for the walls, fresh gilding and marbling, and additional scagliola columns to accommodate plaster busts. The fireplaces are made from Derbyshire fossil and the floor is of oak, matching the bookcases in the Octagon, which were installed in 1827.

The Long Gallery celebrates two important aspects of the picture collection: Italian landscapes and family portraits by English artists. At the south end are landscapes painted by Ricci, one of the earliest artists commissioned to decorate the interiors of the house from 1709 to 1711. The dramatic scenes include a shipwreck, a storm and an artist sketching by a rocky waterfall. The gallery also contains marble-topped tables and a suite of furniture reupholstered in a crimson moiré silk. As a neoclassical display space, the gallery now looks more like it did when completed in the early nineteenth century.

In the Octagon are portraits of Elizabeth, the 2nd Countess, by Sir Godfrey Kneller, the 5th Earl by John Hoppner, the 6th Earl by Sir Thomas Lawrence and a double portrait of Rosalind Stanley (future 9th Countess) with her younger sister Kate, painted by Edwin Long (c.1860).

The classical images of Italy have constantly exercised a powerful influence on the English, who have also revered the landscapes of the British Isles. Thus above the Panini *capriccios* hang a set of four landscapes of Castle Howard commissioned by the 5th Earl from William Marlow in the 1770s. They reveal how the house and grounds appeared towards the end of the century. Two of the landscapes are panoramic views of the wider estate, while the other two feature the house prominently. The view of the west front shows Robinson's attic storeys before they were dismantled, as well as an early glimpse of a body of water to the north of the house. The view of the south side depicts the gardens and the slope up into Ray Wood to the east of the house.

ABOVE The north end of the Long Gallery epitomises eighteenth-century Castle Howard as Roman *capriccios* by Panini are balanced by views of the house and grounds by Marlow. Above the fireplace is Pellegrini's portrait of the three daughters of the 3rd Earl.

RECREATING ROME IN YORKSHIRE

At the north end of the Long Gallery is a set six Roman *capriccios* commissioned from Panini by the 4th Earl during his second visit to Italy, in 1738–39; they finally reached Yorkshire in 1741. Five of their frames are decorated with a gilt Greek key pattern, but the sixth picture has a different frame for reasons unknown.

Extremely popular in the eighteenth century, *capriccios* such as these, depicting real buildings in imaginary settings and groupings, were a visual anthology of everything that had been admired on the Grand Tour. The Roman scenes contain a host of features that every self-respecting Tourist and connoisseur would have been familiar with: the Colosseum, the Arch of Constantine, the Pantheon and the Temples of the Forum.

At Castle Howard the memories of the classical world were taken a stage further. Some of the elements in these paintings, such as the Medici Vase and statues of Hercules, Hygeia and the Dying Gaul, also exist in marble, bronze, lead or plaster versions, either in the house or in the grounds. The 3rd, 4th and 5th Earls were not simply content with pictorial reminders of classical Rome: their many acquisitions illustrate their desire to recreate the atmosphere of ancient Rome in their home.

BELOW *The Baths of Caracalla, Rome* by Paolo Panini, 1740. Among the statues in the arcade is the figure of Hercules. Two other versions of this famous statue exist at Castle Howard: a lead copy in the grounds, purchased by the 3rd Earl in 1723, and a small sixteenth-century bronze bought by the 4th Earl (below left).

The Picture Collection

The core of the picture collection was gathered by three generations in less than a century. The 3rd, 4th and 5th Earls purchased widely as they toured Europe, but they also commissioned English artists and frequented London sale rooms.

The 3rd Earl began to collect pictures, tapestries and sculpture during the early years of the eighteenth century with a view to furnishing his newly built house. Typical of this is the work of Marco Ricci, whose paintings filled the interiors with landscapes; many of these were overdoor or overmantel pieces that were lost in the 1940 fire. In recent years a number of his other landscapes have been cleaned and put back on display, among the largest being *View of the Mall* in London.

ABOVE *View of the Mall* by Marco Ricci, c.1710.

Although the 4th Earl was a passionate collector of antique sculpture, his love of Italy also manifested itself in his purchase of paintings by Paolo Panini, Francesco Zuccarelli and, most importantly, Canaletto. Nearly 50 pictures attributed to Canaletto were once in the collection, listed in old inventories simply as 'View of Venice'. Research has now shown that a number of these were by Canaletto's contemporaries, his nephew Bernardo Bellotto and Michele Marieschi. Some views began to be sold in the late nineteenth century, more were destroyed in the fire and the remainder auctioned in 1944. Today three pictures from this once vast Venetian collection remain at Castle Howard.

BELOW *The Campo San Stefano, Venice* by Bernardo Bellotto, c.1739.

Like his father and his grandfather before him, the 5th Earl visited Italy and continued the tradition of purchasing pictures. In addition to acquiring Italian Old Master paintings, he patronised English artists: Sir Joshua Reynolds , Johan Zoffany, Thomas Gainsborough, Francis Wheatley and George Stubbs.

RIGHT *Frederick Howard, 5th Earl of Carlisle, as a Young Boy* by Sir Joshua Reynolds, 1758.

BELOW LEFT *The 5th Earl of Carlisle with Members of his Family and Household in Phoenix Park, Dublin* by Francis Wheatley, 1781.

BELOW RIGHT *A Favourite Horse of Frederick, 5th Earl of Carlisle* by George Stubbs, 1773.

ABOVE *Portrait of an Old Woman*, said to be his mother, by Leandro Bassano, date unknown.

ABOVE *The Dukes of Ferrara* by Girolamo Bedoli, c.1540.

BELOW *Portrait of a Gentleman*, thought to be a self-portrait, by Annibale Carracci, date unknown.

ABOVE *Salome with the Head of John the Baptist* by Peter Paul Rubens, early seventeenth century.

The climax to his collecting occurred in 1798 when he acquired 13 Italian Old Masters and two Dutch and Flemish pictures from the Orleans Collection sale in London. Among these were paintings by Leandro Bassano, Girolamo Bedoli, Domenico Feti, the Carracci family, Orazio Gentileschi and Titian. In 1805 the 5th Earl published the first-ever printed catalogue of the collection, listing 111 paintings with brief descriptive notes composed by himself. By the time of the fourth edition in 1845 the number of pictures had grown to 274.

The final chapter in the history of the collection began with the 9th Earl and Countess. As a painter himself, the earl moved in Pre-Raphaelite circles and commissioned portraits by Frederic, Lord Leighton and George Frederic Watts. During these years the link between Castle Howard and Italy revived, albeit in a different manner to before. In 1865 the earl met the Italian artist Giovanni Costa, and under his tutelage he developed his talents as a landscape painter in oils and watercolour. The two men eventually formed the Etruscan School of painters in 1883–84, which was renowned for its depictions of the Italian campagna.

The Chapel

In common with many country houses, Castle Howard has a private chapel. This interior in the west wing was first fashioned by Robinson with two screens of columns and an elaborate ceiling based on Holbein's designs for the Royal Chapel at St James's Palace. Originally designed as a dining room, it began to be used for worship at the end of the eighteenth century.

Between 1870 and 1875 it was extensively altered by Edward Howard, Lord Lanerton, who lived at Castle Howard during the illness of his brother, the 8th Earl. The Newcastle architect Robert Johnson lowered the floor level, and the space was redecorated by the firm of Morris & Co. at the urging of

OPPOSITE The chapel is Anglican, as it has always been. It is used for services and for family marriages, baptisms and funerals.

LEFT The picture of Christ at the pillar, above the altar, and the murals were painted by Wyndham Hope Hughes and his assistant to the designs of Charles Eamer Kempe.

LEFT AND BELOW On the north wall above the windows is a scene of angels in a garden painted in a *trompe l'oeil* effect to mimic a textile hanging. On the opposite wall figures from the Old Testament flank a scene of the Annunciation by Kempe.

BELOW Two of Burne-Jones's windows illustrating the Annunciation (left) and the Adoration of the Magi (right). The upper panels depict the symbols of the four evangelists: Matthew (angel), Mark (lion), Luke (ox) and John (eagle).

Lanerton's nephew, the young George Howard (later the 9th Earl). The result was an extraordinary interior decorated with marble floors and an ornate plaster ceiling. One effect of lowering the floor and installing stained glass was to create an entirely enclosed space with no external reference, so that one's gaze would be focused exclusively on the aesthetic and spiritual impact of the interior.

The stained-glass windows designed by Burne-Jones were executed by Morris & Co. in 1872 and illustrate scenes from the life of Christ: the Annunciation, Nativity, Adoration of the Magi and Flight from Egypt. A fifth scene, the Resurrection, was originally planned for the window at the eastern end, but this was eventually decorated with a geometric flower pattern. The windows are hinged on the left side in such a way that the casement can be angled inwards and back-lit by the north-facing windows behind.

William Morris Decoration

Castle Howard is celebrated as a great eighteenth-century house, but it has many important later chapters, such as the transformation of the chapel into the Arts and Crafts style at the end of the nineteenth century. The 9th Earl and Countess of Carlisle numbered among their close personal friends William Morris, Edward Burne-Jones, the architect Philip Webb and a host of other artistic figures from the Pre-Raphaelite circle. Burne-Jones tutored the earl as an artist and there are more than 400 letters from him in the archives. The Howards also spent time in Italy with William and Jane Morris and some of their children. The couple were among some of the most enthusiastic patrons of Morris & Co., making frequent purchases of wallpapers, textiles and furniture to decorate all three of their family homes, Castle Howard, Naworth Castle and No. 1 Palace Green in London, which had been built for them by Webb in the late 1860s.

LIBRARY, CASTLE HOWARD

ABOVE Red and gold 'Sunflower' pattern wallpaper by Morris & Co. In the 1880s the Long Gallery was redecorated by the 9th Countess using 170 rolls of the paper in a dark red colour scheme. Elsewhere in the house she redecorated nearly a dozen rooms with Morris wallpapers.

RIGHT A late nineteenth-century postcard view of the Long Gallery, when it was known as the library, with its red-papered walls. This scheme lasted until the 1960s.

ABOVE A set of eight embroidered panels, depicting women inspired by Geoffrey Chaucer's medieval poem *The Legend of Good Women*, was created for Morris's home in Kent, the Red House. In 1887 the 9th Countess purchased three of the panels and had them made into this oak-framed screen.

RIGHT AND FAR RIGHT
Both Burne-Jones and Morris visited the Howards at Naworth Castle in the 1880s with their families. These small pencil portraits by the 9th Earl are among many

informal sketches that he made of his friends, usually in the evenings when they were reading, drawing or conversing together.

Bedrooms and Dressing Rooms

The bedrooms at Castle Howard are arranged throughout the house on the principal floor and on the upper levels in the central block and two wings, not forgetting the attic and basement areas for servants in past centuries.

The suite in the west wing dates from the late eighteenth century, when Robinson's interiors were completed, and housed the family apartments for the 6th Earl and his wife Georgiana after their marriage in 1801. These rooms are used by family and guests today when the house is closed to the public.

A watercolour by John Russell shows Georgiana as an infant holding a rattle (there is a nearly identical rattle displayed underneath); a second portrait, by Robert Thorburn in 1853, depicts her as a Victorian matriarch. Elsewhere on the walls hang numerous pictures of her children and their families. In the adjacent dressing room the eighteenth-century Dutch opflaptafel is a reminder of how

BELOW Lady Georgiana's bedroom is dominated by a large four-poster bed dating from c.1780, crowned with feather plumes and the uprights painted with a delicate oak-leaf pattern.

ABOVE The Chinese-style wallpaper and blanc de chine figures on the mantelpiece are a reminder that in the eighteenth century parts of the house were decorated by Isabella, the 4th Countess, in a chinoiserie style.

such rooms were serviced in an era before modern plumbing: this washstand would be emptied several times a day by servants who entered the rooms not through their connecting doors but from the corridor behind. In 2022–23 modern plumbing and heating were installed, using period-style fittings. In 2025 the room was decorated with a hand-painted 'Abbotsford' Chinese-style wallpaper given by de Gournay featuring a garden scene with figures, trees and birds, and with fabrics by Colefax and Fowler.

The second suite of rooms was for Georgiana's husband, the 6th Earl. In the nineteenth century the bed was radically altered: originally much taller and with a domed canopy, when it was moved to this room with its lower ceiling the upper portion was cut down and replaced with a tiered finish. The dressing room is decorated with a late nineteenth-century rose-branch wallpaper purchased by Rosalind, the 9th Countess, in 1884.

LEFT The walls in the 6th Earl's dressing room are hung with Dutch flower paintings by Jean Baptiste Monnoyer.

ABOVE The 6th Earl's bedroom, known as the Castle Howard bedroom, was redecorated in 2025 with gathered gold taffeta silk from Italy. The set of satinwood furniture, comprising pelmets, chairs, commodes and a table, is by the Georgian cabinetmaker John Linnell, who was commissioned by the 5th Earl in 1778-79. The bed is hung with a red silk damask from the Lelièvre mill in France.

RIGHT In the High South, the Admiral's Room was decorated in 2023 by Remy Renzullo with an indienne 'Tree of Life' fabric. The original design in the collection was reproduced by the firm Watts 1874.

BELOW Beyond the 6th Earl's and Countess's rooms is the Archbishop's Room, with another four-poster bed and walls hung with a Japanese goose-patterned wallpaper from the 1880s. Both this and the Admiral's Room are occasionally open to the public.

Redecoration and Refurbishment

Descriptions of Castle Howard's interiors repeatedly comment on the lavish decoration. Colour schemes, textiles, wallpapers and furniture have been refreshed by each generation, looking to fashion and modernise the house to their own taste.

The rise of picture collecting in the eighteenth century meant that tapestry hangings were gradually replaced by a collection of landscapes and Old Master paintings acquired on the Grand Tour. The growing trade between Europe and Asia also sparked an enthusiasm for imported porcelain, silks, wallpapers and lacquer furniture.

Chinoiserie tapestries were hung in the house as early as 1720, and Isabella, the 4th Countess, redecorated four rooms with hand-painted Chinese wallpapers. A century later Georgiana, the 6th Countess, purchased wallpapers from Duppa & Collins in London as well as textiles and carpets. By the 1880s it was the turn of Rosalind, the 9th Countess, to refresh the house: 'We must make things ship-shape, and dilapidated finery is not pleasant to see,' she declared, and turned to the firm of Morris & Co. for new fashions in furniture, rugs, tapestries, textiles and wallpapers. She also patronised fashionable London stores such as Liberty and Swan & Edgar and embraced the craze for 'Oriental' design. This cycle of renewal continued when George and Lady Cecilia Howard moved into the house at the end of the 1940s, and more recently with refurbishments carried out by Francis Terry, Remy Renzullo and Alec Cobbe, commissioned by Nicholas and Victoria Howard, who have maintained the family tradition of updating the interiors.

OPPOSITE FAR LEFT
Wallpapers ordered for Castle Howard from Duppa & Collins in the 1820s.

OPPOSITE Japanese 'Goose' pattern wallpaper purchased in the 1880s by the 9th Countess, with a distinctive design of geese flying among roses and lilies.

BELOW Hanging 'Autumn' in the Tapestry Drawing Room.

RIGHT, TOP TO BOTTOM
Following the creation of a new lobby for the Castle Howard bedroom, it was decorated with unused lengths of embossed wallpaper purchased by the 9th Countess in 1886.

Hanging the de Gournay Chinese-style wallpaper in Lady Georgiana's Dressing Room in 2025.

Modelling the scallop shell in plaster for the fireplace in the Tapestry Drawing Room.

Gilding the frieze in the Tapestry Drawing Room.

Behind Closed Doors

There is more to Castle Howard than the grand state rooms, dramatic corridors, painted hall and bedrooms, sumptuously decorated and filled with treasures as they are. There are 'hidden' interiors including cellars, former servants' rooms and the entire west wing basement below ground. Elsewhere there are spiral staircases that lead up to the circular gallery in the dome, which offers vertiginous views down into the hall and a magnificent 360-degree panorama of the grounds, and there are also burnt-out spaces, not to mention acres of roof. The shell of the south-east wing is a stark illustration of the ravages of the fire but also points to the possibilities for restoration. All of these interiors tell a different story to the rest of the house. These areas are open at times for behind the scenes guided tours.

BELOW LEFT The basement-level ruins in the south-east wing. This room, with its arched niches, was formerly known as the Colonnade. On the floor above was the Little Gallery and at roof level were two small domes. All were lost in 1940.

BELOW The gallery in the dome at the very top of the house. Eight tall windows flood this upper area with daylight.

ABOVE The basement corridor runs for 60 metres through the centre of the building. Halfway along is the bell that would sound when people were at the front door.

RIGHT A bell board in the upper level of the west wing that would summon servants to rooms in this part of the house.

Archives

Castle Howard is filled with treasures of many sorts, but perhaps the most important, and least visible, is the large archive. It is the engine room of history. This priceless assembly of written records testifies to a family who never threw anything away. Among the documents are account books and ledgers, letter-books and journals, and estate papers dealing with land, farming, woodlands and villages. There are family sketchbooks and photograph albums; there is correspondence from Vanbrugh and Hawksmoor, and papers detailing the cost of building Castle Howard; and there are household bills and room inventories that are an invaluable guide to how the house was furnished and provisioned at various moments. These precious records enable a host of stories to be told about the house, family, estate and collections.

OPPOSITE

ABOVE LEFT An illustrated letter from Burne-Jones to the 9th Earl, thanking him for the gift of a waistcoat.

ABOVE RIGHT A sketch by the 9th Earl showing family holidays in the 1890s.

BELOW LEFT The bill for the marble copy of the Dying Gaul, purchased in Rome by the 5th Earl in 1768.

BELOW RIGHT A recipe for preserving pineapples from a 'Book of Receipts' compiled in the 1740s by the 4th Countess.

LEFT The 9th Earl and Countess with their children and grandchildren on the north steps of the house, c.1890.

...them.

So glad you like Stowell. who is a character, inexhaustibly interesting & unceasingly amusing. all our loves to you both. we shall be so glad when you come back. always your most affect. ned.

This does no manner of justice to the waistcoat the only distressing point that I feel

all other parts of dress disreputable by comparison, so that I am afraid people may think I have stolen it.

Charles doing up the overalls for the last time on the steamer.

The Fiddle is in danger at Perth.

The Honble The Earl of Carlisle to Thos. Jenkins

for two Landskips by Gas: Poussin	£35
two Small Landskips by Sal: Rosa	10
a Copy of the Fighting Gladiator	25
for a Copy of a Venus by Ludovico Them	40. Zec:
for three Rings	16. Zec:
for a Bustino Antique	6. Zec:
a Small Sarcophagus	5. Zec:
for a Frame to the Copy of the Venus	8. Zec:
for a Stesus	5. pauls

makes at the Exchange of 42 per pound — £36-15

Total One Hundred & Six Pounds fifteen Shillings £106-15

on Account of the Honble Charles Fox — £-42-00

Total One Hundred & forty Eight Pounds £148-15 fifteen Shillings Sterlg — P.S. Rome June the 30. 1768

for a Copy from Raphael — £20-00

for two Bustini — £7-00

Total — £175-15

Received the Contents and all Demands Rome July the 4 - 1768 — Thos. Jenkins.

To preserve Pine Apples +

Take the Apples and pare them close to the Meat and cut them in Slices about the thickness of half a Crown to a Pound of Apple one Pound and half of double refined Sugar finely beaten strew the Sugar on them as you slice them till it is all used then let them stand till the Sugar is all dissolved then put them into a preserving Pan and boil them till they are tender and clear put them into a China Bowl and let them stand till the next Day then warm them but not to Boil every day for nine days then lay them on China Plates to dry in a slow Oven turning them three or four times a day till they are dry.

Filming at Castle Howard:
From Brideshead to Bridgerton

Castle Howard has regularly appeared on screen. In the 1960s George Howard recognised its potential as a location to raise funds towards ongoing restoration and to bring Castle Howard to the attention of audiences worldwide.

In 1965 the house was the setting for the comedy *Lady L*, directed by Peter Ustinov and starring Sophia Loren and David Niven. Ten years later Stanley Kubrick arrived to direct *Barry Lyndon*, his film adaptation of William Makepeace Thackeray's novel, and Castle Howard became 'Castle Hackton'.

But it was the Granada Television production of Evelyn Waugh's novel *Brideshead Revisited*, broadcast in 1981, that catapulted Castle Howard to global fame. The 11-episode drama remains a high point in the annals of television history, featuring established stars such as Laurence Olivier, Claire Bloom and Ralph Richardson, as well as introducing younger actors like Jeremy Irons, Anthony Andrews and Diana Quick. The enduring appeal of the series is that the story is in many ways about a love affair with a house, and Castle Howard doubled for the Flyte family home, Brideshead Castle (itself distinguished by a grand dome in the story). The novel was filmed at Castle Howard a second time in 2008 with Miramax Films.

Other television appearances have included P.D. James's eighteenth-century murder mystery *Death Comes to Pemberley* (2013); as Clyvedon Castle, the ancestral home of the Duke of Hastings in the first series

of *Bridgerton* (2020); and in 2018 the Arctic Monkeys filmed their music video for 'Four Out of Five' at Castle Howard. While the house has appeared in many fictional guises, it always remains uniquely identifiable as Castle Howard.

ABOVE Sophia Loren as Lady L in 1965.

TOP The central characters from the Granada Television production of *Brideshead Revisited*: left to right, Sebastian Flyte (Anthony Andrews), Julia Flyte (Diana Quick) and Charles Ryder (Jeremy Irons).

ABOVE The Netflix smash hit *Bridgerton*, set in Regency England, follows the lives and loves of the Bridgerton family. Early in the story Daphne (Phoebe Dynevor) marries the Duke of Hastings (Regé-Jean Page) and the couple arrive at his family home Clyvedon, where they are greeted by housekeeper Mrs Colson (Pippa Haywood).

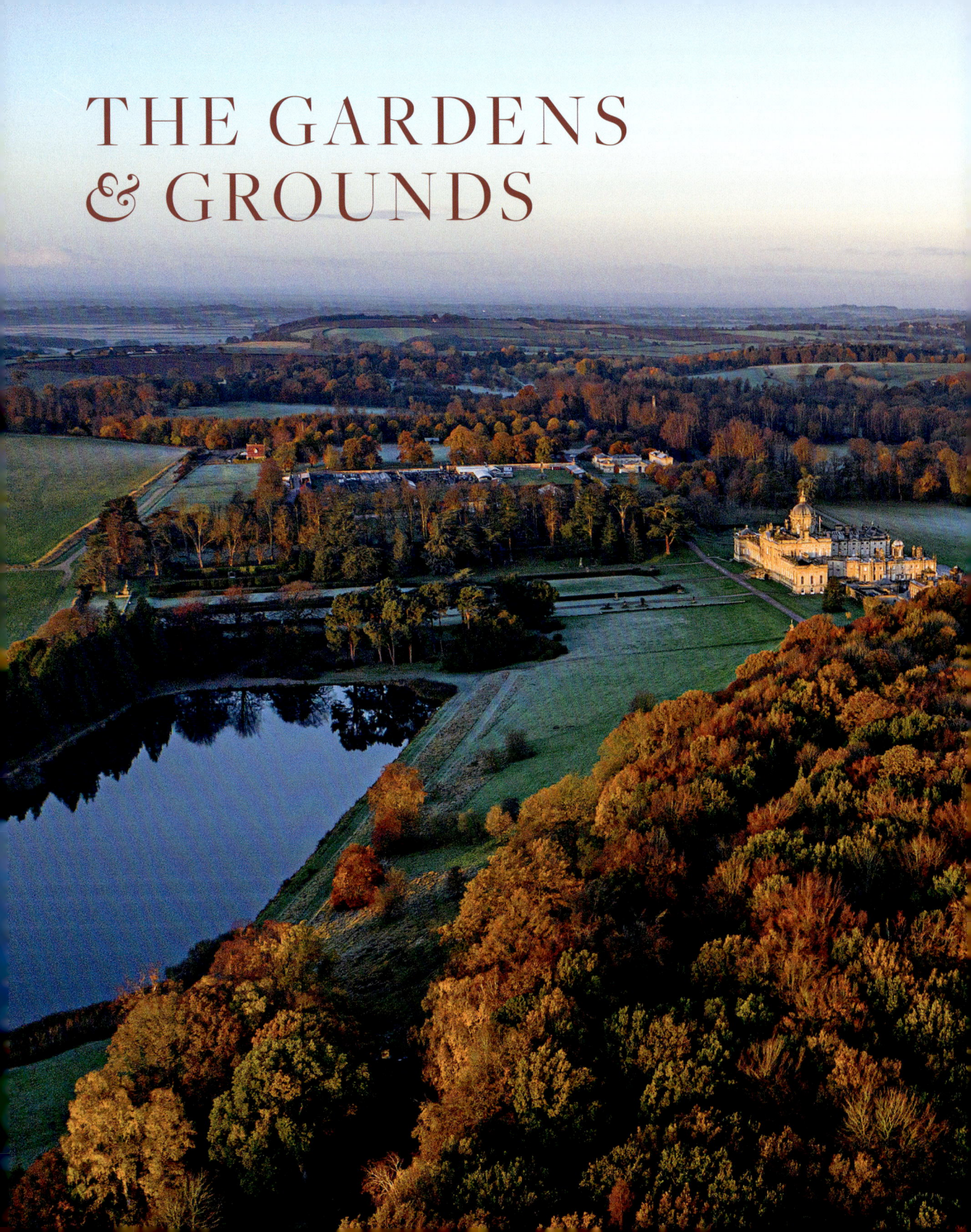

THE GARDENS
& GROUNDS

Introduction

The grounds at Castle Howard have always impressed with their splendour and variety. In 1732 one visitor remarked that 'the chief excellency of these gardens consists in the infinite variety you see in them, so that you may very properly call it not one but ten different gardens'.

The same holds true today, and visitors can enjoy extensive walks through woodlands, formal gardens, along terraces or beside water and view the buildings and sculpture in the wider landscape. Everywhere a different note from history is sounded: while Castle Howard is famous for its early eighteenth-century landscape, as laid out by the 3rd Earl, Vanbrugh and Hawksmoor, there are elements of Victorian intervention as well as more recent restoration and development.

Laid out in an informal manner, Castle Howard was in the vanguard of the eighteenth-century English landscape garden tradition. It has been fashioned on a heroic scale with expansive views and distant eye-catchers, all of which take advantage of the undulating topography of the Howardian Hills.

The temples, monuments, terraces and lakes date from the eighteenth century, but the fountains and waterways were installed between 1850 and 1865. Ray Wood was replanted in the 1970s and the Rose Garden a few years later, while the waterways were restored and refashioned at the end of the twentieth century.

OPPOSITE Two views of Castle Howard commissioned from the Flemish painter Hendrik de Cort in c.1800 by the 5th Earl to hang in his London home. One view is from the south-east, with Hawksmoor's mausoleum in the foreground (above); the other from the north-west, with the Great Lake in the foreground and the house and Ray Wood beyond (below).

'If our first parents, after being turned out of the Garden of Eden, had been immediately placed upon this spot of ground, they would have concluded that they had only exchanged one Paradise for another.'

JOHN TRACY ATKYNS, 1732

Ray Wood

Standing on the site of an ancient woodland, Ray Wood has undergone several transformations during the past three centuries. In the eighteenth century it was renowned for its natural style: the 3rd Earl refused to tame it with a geometry of straight rides in a star-shaped pattern. Instead he favoured a design of irregular, serpentine pathways widely praised by contemporaries. So mazy were these paths that members of the Howard family are said to have got lost in them once.

Ray Wood was filled with lead statues and pavilions; there were also fountains and a cascade that Hawksmoor designed. But these features disappeared by the middle of the eighteenth century, and all that remains of the waterworks is the hilltop reservoir, which was rebuilt in the 1850s to supply both of the fountains installed by Nesfield.

BELOW The hilltop reservoir in Ray Wood, which holds 2.75 million litres of water.

ABOVE Carved on the face of the pedestal in the centre of the reservoir is a host of aquatic creatures and plants. Normally these figures are submerged beneath the waterline, but the top course is often visible when the water level drops.

RIGHT A detail from an estate map of 1773, marking in some of the serpentine pathways in Ray Wood. Few, if any, of the statues and pavilions remained in the wood by this date and the waterworks had been dismantled.

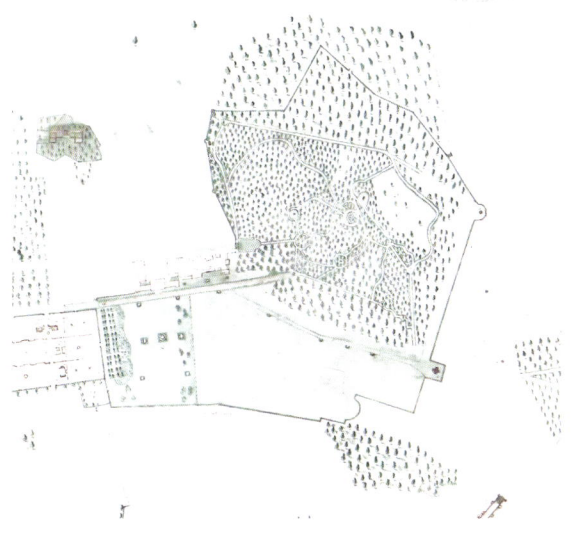

Two typical views of Ray Wood in springtime, with an exuberant spectrum of colours as the rhododendrons and azaleas blossom beneath the tree canopy that has been selectively thinned over the years.

During the Second World War Ray Wood was clear-felled, leaving the hilltop completely bare. Replanting began in the 1950s, and then the wood was remodelled in the 1970s by George Howard and James Russell, who had come to Castle Howard from Sunningdale Nurseries. They decided to reinstate the winding pathways as a framework for new ornamental plantings in a woodland setting. Today, under a canopy of oak, beech and sweet chestnuts, the wood stretches across 25 acres with a collection of trees and shrubs gathered from all over the world, including magnolias, hydrangeas, viburnums, maples and rowans. The rhododendrons and azaleas are well suited to the acidic soil and in spring offer a vivid spectacle, but the autumn hues are equally rich and varied. Ray Wood is recognised for its nationally important collections, with rare and unusual plants propagated to ensure they will continue to thrive. It is managed by the Castle Howard Arboretum Trust, a charity formed in 1994, as a collaboration between Castle Howard and the Royal Botanic Gardens, Kew.

South Parterre and Atlas Fountain

The South Parterre was laid out c.1715–25, when the 3rd Earl and Vanbrugh established a parterre of plain grass with raised terraces and planted it with obelisks, urns, statues and a 15-metre column in what was an architectural garden. These dominant features extended the Baroque style of the house into the surrounding landscape.

Most of the features had been removed by the 1850s when the landscape gardener Nesfield installed the Atlas Fountain as the centrepiece to his geometrically patterned parterre. Carved from Portland stone by the sculptor John Thomas, the fountain features a crouching Atlas bearing a heavy globe on his shoulders, which is decorated with gilded signs of the zodiac. He is surrounded by reclining tritons blowing jets of water through conch shells.

BELOW *A Perspective View of Castle Howard Taken from the Inn* attributed to George Lambert and Philip Mercier, c.1750. The painting shows Hawksmoor's bow window and the two small domes above, before they were demolished to make way for Robinson's west wing. It also provides a glimpse of Vanbrugh's parterre with obelisks and statues. The painting is in the collection at Rokeby Park, Co. Durham, the house built by Robinson for himself.

OPPOSITE BELOW The main spout for the Atlas Fountain issues from the top of the globe. Below there are four jets of water from the surrounding tritons, and the upper basin is ringed with scallop shells that fill and overflow into the main basin beneath.

RIGHT Nesfield's sketch of the water jets of the Atlas Fountain and South Lake fountain in action, which he included in a letter to the 7th Earl when reporting the first successful demonstration of both of his fountains in October 1853.

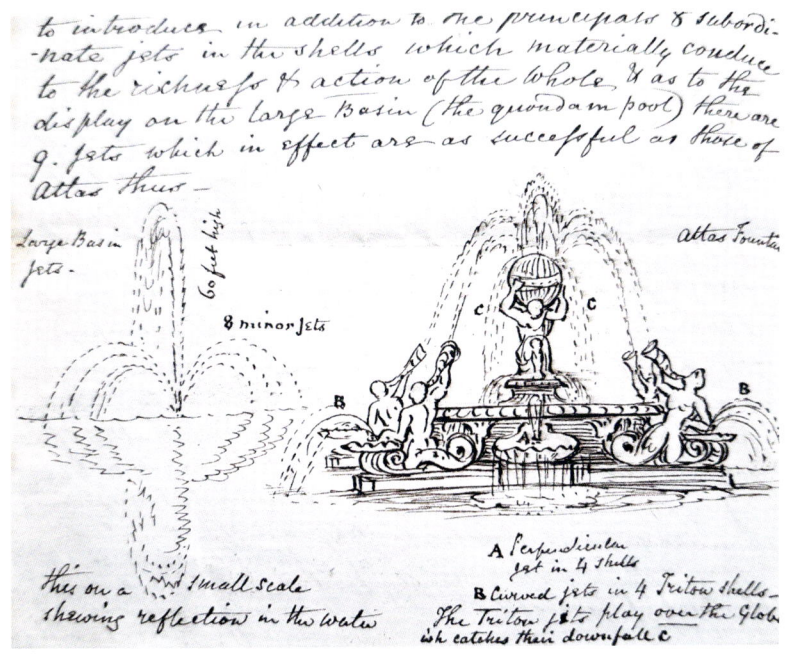

to introduce in addition to the principals & subordi-
-nate jets in the shells which materially conduce
to the richness & action of the Whole & as to the
display on the large Basin (the quondam pool) there are
9 jets which in effect are as successful as those of
Atlas thus —

Large Basin jets.

60 feet high

8 minor jets

Atlas Fountain

A Perpendicular jet in 4 shells
B Curved jets in 4 Triton shells —
The Triton jets play over the Globe
ish catches their downfall c

this on a small scale
shewing reflection in the water

These improvements commissioned by the 7th Earl were costly, and by 1855 Nesfield's initial estimate of £2,000 had risen to a staggering £10,000. Although very fashionable in the middle of the nineteenth century, the manicured parterres of low box hedging, plants and coloured gravel were very expensive to maintain. By the 1880s they had fallen out of fashion and the 9th Countess also objected to the cost of their upkeep. The parterre was simplified into the grass terraces and yew hedges of today.

OPPOSITE The giant figure of Atlas and other sculptural components were transported from London by rail in 1850. Conveniently, the Castle Howard station three miles away had opened a few years earlier. Beneath the fountain basin is a large chamber housing all the hydraulics.

LEFT ABOVE This elevated view of c.1870 reveals how Nesfield's parterre was structured around a geometrical pattern of scrolls, volutes, scallops and crosslets.

LEFT BELOW The South Parterre is still dominated by the Atlas Fountain. Outside the border of yew hedges there remain six eighteenth-century lead statues and an assortment of stone vases and planters for changing flower displays.

Walled Garden

The Walled Garden was laid out in the early years of the eighteenth century as a kitchen garden to the south-west of the house. The brick walls provide shelter and a suitable microclimate for growing plants and all sorts of produce.

Later in the century the garden was doubled in size to its current ten acres. The Gardener's House sat at the centre and to the west there was a series of heated walls with flues. Together with the hothouses and conservatories the garden grew a wide range of exotic produce, including grapes, nectarines and pomegranates. The pineapple and melon pits were located at the western extremity, close to the stables to ensure a ready supply of that essential growing medium: manure. Their distant position from the house also meant that family and guests did not encounter offensive smells.

Today the garden is given over to a mixture of roses, flowers for cutting and vegetables. Other parts of the area are used for events, and in the western portion is the Castle Howard Garden Centre.

OPPOSITE The dipping pond in front of the Gardener's House may look like an ornamental pool with its little statue and fountain in the centre, but it is still used by the gardeners today to fill watering cans.

BELOW LEFT Lady Cecilia's Rose Garden was established in 1975 in memory of George Howard's wife, Lady Cecilia; the Sundial and Venus Gardens were laid out a few years later.

BELOW RIGHT In 1705 the Satyr Gate entrance was built, with its vigorous lion and satyr masks and stone baskets of ornamental flowers, carved by the Yorkshire mason Samuel Carpenter with ironwork by John Gardom.

South Lake

The South Lake below the Temple Terrace was constructed in the early 1720s. New River beyond was widened from a natural stream a decade later, prior to the construction of New River Bridge in the 1740s. Plans for a lake to the north of the House (first mooted by Hawksmoor) did not materialise until the 1790s, when the 5th Earl commissioned the Yorkshire-born engineer William Chapman to create the Great Lake.

The South Lake was refashioned by Nesfield at the same time as he installed the Prince of Wales Fountain there in 1850. Ten years later the empty area between the lake and New River was formalised with the construction of the Cascade, Temple Hole basin and the Waterfall. These features remained after the 9th Countess removed much of Nesfield's scheme, but they fell into disrepair during the twentieth century until they were fully restored in the late 1980s.

Both of Nesfield's fountains are gravity-fed from Ray Wood Reservoir, and the overflow from the Atlas Fountain feeds the subsidiary jets, or feathers, for the Prince of Wales Fountain. The southern waterways flow out of New River, passing an old watermill a mile away before finally reaching the River Derwent.

BELOW According to the sixteenth-century historian William Camden, the name Henderskelfe is derived from the term 'hundred skell', referring to the many natural springs in the area. Consequently it was not long before these abundant water sources were exploited for ornamental purposes: thus all the lakes and ponds at Castle Howard are artificial.

HOW THE WATERWAYS WORK

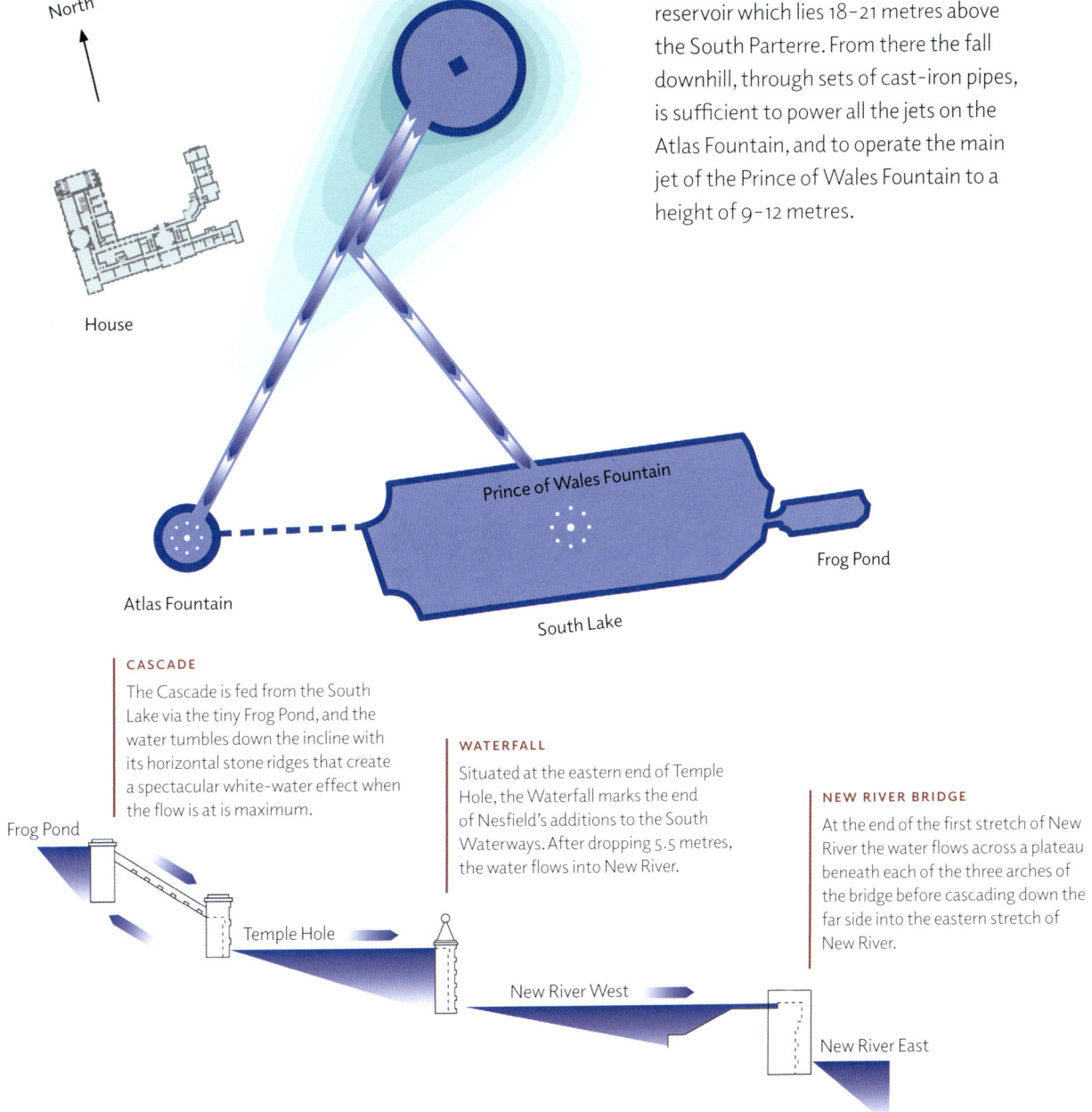

Water is pumped from a local stream to the north of Ray Wood into the hilltop reservoir which lies 18-21 metres above the South Parterre. From there the fall downhill, through sets of cast-iron pipes, is sufficient to power all the jets on the Atlas Fountain, and to operate the main jet of the Prince of Wales Fountain to a height of 9-12 metres.

Ray Wood Reservoir

North

House

Prince of Wales Fountain

Frog Pond

Atlas Fountain

South Lake

CASCADE

The Cascade is fed from the South Lake via the tiny Frog Pond, and the water tumbles down the incline with its horizontal stone ridges that create a spectacular white-water effect when the flow is at is maximum.

WATERFALL

Situated at the eastern end of Temple Hole, the Waterfall marks the end of Nesfield's additions to the South Waterways. After dropping 5.5 metres, the water flows into New River.

NEW RIVER BRIDGE

At the end of the first stretch of New River the water flows across a plateau beneath each of the three arches of the bridge before cascading down the far side into the eastern stretch of New River.

Frog Pond

Temple Hole

New River West

New River East

Temple of the Four Winds and Sculpture

In 1724 Vanbrugh sent some designs for a pavilion for the south-east corner of Ray Wood, and he was soon pleased to learn that the earl had 'at last inclined to the Temple with four Porticoes'.

Known originally as the Temple of Diana, the building - a cube with a dome and porticoes on each elevation - is modelled in part on Andrea Palladio's sixteenth-century Villa Rotonda in Vicenza. When Vanbrugh died in 1726 the temple was unfinished, and Hawksmoor was entrusted with the completion.

The temple lies at the eastern end of the terrace that extends from the house, which before 1699 was part of the main street for the medieval village of Henderskelfe. Used as a place for socialising, there is a cellar beneath which servants would store and prepare refreshment for society above. Described by Vanbrugh as his 'belvedere temple', it commands impressive views in all directions. To the north, a quarter of a mile away, is the site of Hawksmoor's Temple of Venus, demolished in the 1940s.

OPPOSITE The temple stands on a raised grass platform, bounded by walls and with steps leading into the parkland.

LEFT The interior was decorated with a mix of scagliola and Rococo-style plasterwork by the Swiss stuccoist Francesco Vassali in the 1730s. The motif of four runs though the building: four statues on the outside steps, four busts above the doorways, four bearded masks in the upper lantern and four gilded faces in the plasterwork. The floor is finished in a mosaic patterning known as Cosmati work, named after the Italian craftsmen famous for this technique.

Vanbrugh's temple narrowly avoided a similar fate as it too deteriorated in the early twentieth century. It was restored in 1955 as one of the first projects undertaken by George Howard on his return after the war, when the dome was rebuilt with new timbers and lined with lead. Once the outer structure had been completed, the internal plasterwork was recreated and regilded.

ABOVE The upper section of the dome has four octagonal windows with a central lantern above that illuminate the detail. Seen from the ground-floor level, the circle of the dome is perfectly set in the square design of the lower portion of the building.

LEAD SCULPTURE

Lead sculptures filled the grounds in the eighteenth century, an era when they could be manufactured inexpensively rather than as individual commissions from a sculptor. Modelled on figures from antiquity, the statues were purchased by the 3rd Earl from the London yards of John Nost and Andrew Carpenter. The Temple Terrace is now lined with figures of Bacchus, Hercules, Meleager, Antinous and the Borghese Gladiator. The four statues on the steps of the temple, purchased in 1731, are of Roman empresses.

The entire collection was restored in the 1990s with grant aid from English Heritage. Damaged sections were repaired, missing pieces replaced and internal frames renewed. New versions of two important double groups that had disappeared from the South Parterre – Hercules and Antaeus, and Pluto and Proserpine – were commissioned to stand on Hawksmoor's giant pedestals. Today Castle Howard has one of the largest collections of lead sculpture in Britain.

BELOW The Farnese Hercules (left), supplied by Andrew Carpenter in 1723, and the Borghese Gladiator (right) by John Cheere in the 1750s.

The Mausoleum

During the 1720s, after a quarter of a century of continuous building projects, the 3rd Earl's thoughts turned towards death. 'I do design to build a burial place near my seat of Castle Howard, where I desire to be layed', he instructed. He discussed his thoughts with Vanbrugh and Hawksmoor, who both encouraged the idea of a monumental building in the landscape. What resulted was part tomb and part temple.

Its design was based on a number of Roman buildings ancient and modern, such as the tomb of Cecilia Metella, built in the first century BC, and Donato Bramante's sixteenth-century Tempietto di San Pietro in Montorio in Rome. Both are examples of cylindrical buildings. Hawksmoor took this circular form and created a monumental structure standing on a square podium, ringed by 20 gigantic Doric columns.

OPPOSITE The ceiling of the chapel rises 21 metres into the air. The carved decoration is by two Yorkshire masons, Charles Mitley and Edward Raper, and includes cherubims' heads and acanthus leaves on the capitals to the eight Corinthian columns. There are 144 carved panels radiating from a huge central boss.

LEFT Like many buildings at Castle Howard, the siting of the mausoleum in the landscape enhances its impact. It is visible from the house, as well as from other vantage points. It acts as a memento mori, for it is both an architectural and a dynastic monument.

Situated nearly a mile away from the house, the building was begun in 1728 and not completed until the 1740s, after the deaths of both Hawksmoor and the 3rd Earl. Work was dogged by misfortune, intervention and argument, as the 3rd Earl's son Lord Morpeth, his son-in-law Sir Thomas Robinson and the architectural patron Lord Burlington urged various modifications to Hawksmoor's design. These included the proportions of the colonnade, the addition of steps on the east side and the surrounding bastion wall, which was eventually built by the architect Daniel Garrett.

Standing high above New River on a hill known as Mount Sion, and rising 27 metres into the air, the mausoleum was justly celebrated as 'the noblest invention of them all'. Inside, a spectacular ceiling soars above the chapel. The upper storey is lit by large windows and supported on eight fluted columns with acanthus-leaf capitals. There are pews and lecterns at the lower level. Beneath is the crypt, which contains 63 niches, or loculi, for housing coffins.

Visitors have been awed and intrigued by the mausoleum: Walpole declared it was tempting enough to be buried alive inside; Prince Hermann von Pückler-

ABOVE LEFT AND RIGHT
The floor is decorated with a radiating pattern of flowerheads set in brass inlays.

RIGHT The 3rd Earl was first buried in the local parish church at Bulmer, but six years later he was interred in the crypt where a simple inscription marks his final resting place.

Muskau likened the vault to a gigantic beehive; and for the poet John Betjeman it was a reminder that all things must pass. The mausoleum is still the burial place of the Howard family, and after nine generations the vault is less than half full.

DESIGNS FOR THE AFTERLIFE

During the design and building process Hawksmoor corresponded regularly with the 3rd Earl, citing examples of ancient temples and tombs and sending numerous drawings for his approval. Initially an arcade was proposed, but he also submitted a comparative drawing for an arcade and a colonnade, which was eventually agreed upon. As a result of this decision the building became much taller, with a more pronounced vertical profile.

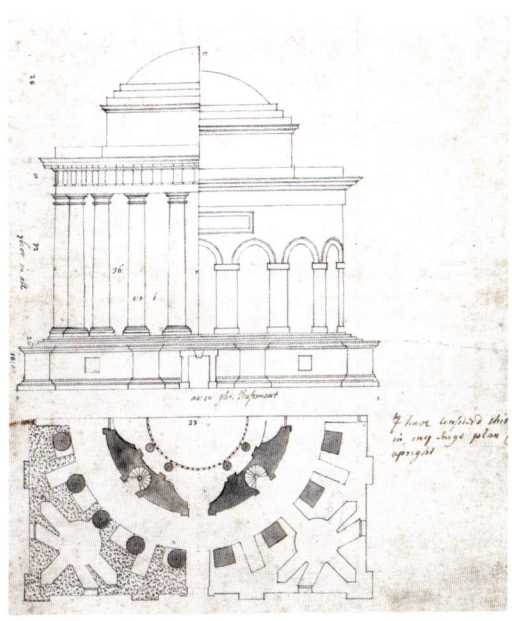

Avenue and Monuments

The estate sits in the rolling Howardian Hills, a designated National Landscape. The approach is along the Avenue, which runs south–north in a straight line for five miles and was laid out at the beginning of the eighteenth century. The southern end is marked by the monument erected to the 7th Earl in 1869–70, which was paid for by public subscription and designed by Frederick Pepys Cockerell.

The central section of the Avenue is planted with lime trees dating from as early as 1705, although many have been replanted over the years following storms. The southern and northern sections were planted at a later date with beech and chestnut trees respectively. When in leaf the Avenue presents a spectacular green corridor on the approach to Castle Howard, and is also a haven for birds and insect life.

As the road rises and falls, the approach becomes an architectural panorama with teasing glimpses of the pyramid, temple and mausoleum in the distance. The medley of architectural styles includes the Carrmire Gate designed by Hawksmoor in the 1720s, with a central arch, crenellated walls and two turrets. This Gothic or medieval effect gives way to an Egyptian or

OPPOSITE The 7th Earl's monument stands on a stepped square base that is flanked by four knights' helmets and heraldic insignia. The column is decorated with two long garlands and the capital at the top supports a gilded tripod and brazier. Damaged by lightning during the twentieth century, these were reinstated in 2001–2 when the monument was repaired.

BELOW The southern section of the Avenue with the Carrmire Gate, which acts as a gateway and a curtain wall. The section leading to the gatehouse is lined with clumps of beech trees. In the far distance are the North Yorkshire Moors.

IN MEMORY OF

Roman impression as the road ascends to the pyramid arch of the gatehouse
built by Vanbrugh in 1719. Extending either side are the Stray Walls, a series of
mock fortifications with turrets and bastions, built in the 1720s to emphasise
what Vanbrugh called a 'castle air'. The wings to the gatehouse were added
by Robinson in 1756–58, after which the building became an inn.

To the east, on the same ridge, sits Hawksmoor's pyramid, built in 1728.
Inside, it houses a colossal bust of Lord William Howard, the Tudor founder
of this branch of the Howard family. A mile further east, inside Pretty Wood,
are two more monuments by Hawksmoor.

At the head of the drive stands Vanbrugh's obelisk, built in 1714–15 and
rising 21 metres high. It carries two sets of inscriptions. The first, in Latin,
commemorates the victories of the 1st Duke of Marlborough. The second, on
the west side and in English, was composed by the 3rd Earl when much of the
building and landscaping had been completed. It was written with posterity
in mind and is the clearest statement possible of the 3rd Earl's aspirations for
himself and his family.

IF TO PERFECTION THESE PLANTATIONS RISE
IF THEY AGREEABLY MY HEIRS SURPRISE
THIS FAITHFUL PILLAR WILL THEIR AGE DECLARE
AS LONG AS TIME THESE CHARACTERS SHALL SPARE
HERE THEN WITH KIND REMEMBRANCE READ HIS NAME
WHO FOR POSTERITY PERFORM'D THE SAME
CHARLES THE III EARL OF CARLISLE
OF THE FAMILY OF THE HOWARDS
ERECTED A CASTLE WHERE THE OLD CASTLE OF
HENDERSKELFE STOOD, AND CALL'D IT CASTLE HOWARD.
HE LIKEWISE MADE THE PLANTATIONS IN THIS PARK
AND ALL THE OUT-WORKS, MONUMENTS AND OTHER
PLANTATIONS BELONGING TO THE SAID SEAT.
HE BEGAN THESE WORKS
IN THE YEAR MDCCII
ANNO D: MDCCXXXI

The Wider Estate

Beyond the house, gardens and parkland lies the wider estate totalling 8,900 acres, which sits in the middle of the Howardian Hills. The topography is characterised by limestone and sandstone escarpments and ridges, with a range of soil types, varying hydrology and distinct pockets of woodland and habitats. It is a rich and diverse landscape.

Castle Howard has been famous as both a sublime and a productive landscape. In the past prize cattle, rare breeds and model farms were valued as much as architecture, gardens and fountains. Today the estate pursues a variety of enterprises, from agriculture and forestry to a holiday park and let properties, which help generate vital income.

Farming has traditionally been one of the mainstays of country estates and today 4,500 acres are given over to agriculture. The arable operation can include wheat, barley, oats and peas. An Aberdeen Angus beef herd was established in 2003 and now numbers 200 cattle. As part of the transition

BELOW An aerial view of the estate which gives a different perspective: the house is a relatively small feature in the extensive 8,900-acre landscape set in the Howardian Hills and characterised by farmland, woods and lakes.

to regenerative farming there is a commitment to the application of fewer chemicals, so as to improve soil and water quality, as well as experimentation with companion cropping: for example, wheat with legumes, which provides diversity and natural nutrition. While food production is an important element of land management, so too is protection of the environment, and the estate is committed to a strategy that looks to safeguard and enhance natural habitats as part of a programme of nature restoration.

Some 440 acres of marginal farmland have been ring-fenced as the flagship Bog Hall habitat bank that will see the establishment of scrub and grassland mosaics, the restoration of wetlands and reintroduction of beavers, as well as public educational programmes.

These initiatives are spurred by the pressures of climate change, the critical importance of nature restoration and opportunities that have arisen as a consequence of leaving the European Union. While they take advantage of the latest scientific research and new technologies, such as a satellite survey of the entire estate, they are a timely reminder that land management has been an ongoing endeavour for centuries. Thus, back in 1805, the 5th Earl conducted his own trials on the composition of manure.

Forestry is an important activity, with 2,300 acres of woodland managed under a long-term countryside stewardship agreement for commercial timber

production and amenity value. The woods divide between coniferous and deciduous plantations, and harvested timber is used for posts, planking and the furniture trade. In recent years older coniferous plantations have been felled and replanted with native broadleaf species including oak, ash and cherry, but there is always the threat of new pests and diseases such as ash dieback.

The Castle Howard Arboretum lies in parkland to the west of the house and, like Ray Wood, is jointly managed by Castle Howard and the Royal Botanic Gardens, Kew. The 120-acre site was created by George Howard and James Russell between 1975 and 1992, and the collection has grown from specimens that came from Hillier Nurseries in 1979, from expeditions to many temperate parts of the world, and also from Kew. The Arboretum has created wildflower meadows, established a small breeding group of red squirrels and, in 2021, opened a Tree Health Centre offering specialist courses on tree management.

The estate is already carbon neutral thanks to large expanses of woodland, but there are active projects to do more to reduce emissions from operations and visitors. Investments have been made over the years in renewables such as a lake-source heating system and a biomass boiler, and work is underway to develop a water management strategy to tackle the extremes of very wet winters and dry summers: at certain times of the year there is too much water, at others too little.

The visitor operation is a central part of the business, especially during the peak Christmas period. There are retail and food offers, and in 2004

ABOVE LEFT Breeding pairs of curlews on the estate benefit from a reduced mowing policy allowing them to establish ground nests in rough pasture or tall grass. Skylarks are frequently heard, but the cuckoo rarely. A welcome sight is the springtime return of house martins, which build their distinctive nests in the window recesses of the house.

ABOVE RIGHT A pear tree, *Pyrus pyrifolia*, sometimes known as the Sand Pear tree, blossoms in the Arboretum during a warm April.

RIGHT AND BELOW Two aerial views of the habitat bank at Bog Hall, each with the mausoleum at the top of the picture. The first shows how the land looks today. The second is a visualisation of its appearance in a few years' time with wetlands, scrub and wood pasture that will improve biodiversity.

the Castle Howard Farm Shop opened in the Stable Courtyard, selling local produce including traditional-reared beef and lamb. There is also a popular Garden Centre and a Tree Nursery, which sell plants and trees found in the grounds and gardens as well as across the wider estate and landscape.

The estate owns 150 residential properties, many of which are let on the open market, while others have been turned into holiday cottages, attracting visitors to stay longer in the area to the benefit of the local economy. On the north shore of the Great Lake is the Lakeside Holiday Park with 160 lodges in a landscaped setting. Elsewhere former farm holdings have been converted into rural office units, and among the estate villages there are opportunities for pockets of development to help address a local housing shortage.

Castle Howard has always played a vital role in the local economy, employing many people indoors and outdoors. The estate does business with more than 1,000 suppliers and contractors in the area, and it employs around 100 people full-time, with additional part-time or seasonal roles, as well as supporting a growing cohort of volunteers.

The impetus for this range of commercial activity is to secure the future of Castle Howard and to preserve its heritage by generating income for never-ending restoration needs. Many of the buildings are fragile with age and also suffering from climate extremes. They are reaching a critical state and require urgent repair. This cycle of work stretches back to the 1950s, when George Howard signalled his commitment to Castle Howard by opening it to the public and tackling vital restoration projects. Since then the estate has spent the equivalent of £40 million in today's values on restoration and repair, on structures as various as the house, temple, pyramid and mausoleum, and on the natural heritage too, replanting sections of the lime trees in the Avenue and recovering the lakes and waterways.

The challenges remain daunting. As each year goes by the cost of repairs increases, and the likely total to make good these priceless heritage features currently stands at around £90 million. The estate works closely with other heritage, educational and commercial partners, including the World Monuments Fund, Historic England, the Environment Bank, Kew Gardens, the Howardian Hills and Yale University. In 2024 the Castle Howard Foundation was established, a charitable body that will apply to various funds to help address these tasks, as well as supporting arts and cultural programmes and encouraging the preservation of traditional heritage skills.

OPPOSITE Statues of Hercules, Apollo and Atlas look back at the house.

First published in 2025 by
Scala Arts & Heritage Publishers Ltd
43 Great Ormond Street, London WC1N 3HZ, UK
www.scalapublishers.com
An imprint of B. T. Batsford Holdings Ltd

In association with
Castle Howard
York YO60 7DA, UK
www.castlehoward.co.uk

ISBN 978-1-78551-617-7 (hardback)
ISBN 978-1-78551-616-0 (paperback)

Project manager and copy-editor: Linda Schofield
Design by: Peter Dawson, Ronja Rønning, www.gradedesign.com
Printed in China

10 9 8 7 6 5 4 3 2

Scala is represented in UK and Europe by Abrams & Chronicle Books,
Abrams & Chronicle Books, 1st Floor, 22-24 Ely Place, London
EC1N 6TE and 57 rue Gaston Tessier, 75166 Paris, France.

Further information on Castle Howard, including a full
bibliography, can be found on the Castle Howard website:
www.castlehoward.co.uk

Acknowledgements and Photographic Credits

Front cover and pp. 2-3, 4, 24-25, 30 (below), 31, 33, 102-3, 104,
106, 111 (below), 112 (below), 113, 116, 119, 121, 122, 123, 124, 125
(above), 126, 127, 128 (below), 129, 130, 131 (right), 133
(above), 135: Nicholas Howard

Back cover and pp. 7, 17, 36, 37, 38, 43, 44, 45, 46-47, 48, 50,
51, 53, 55, 56, 57, 58, 59, 60, 63, 64, 65, 67, 68, 70, 71, 73, 74,
75 (above), 78, 84, 85, 86, 90, 91, 92, 93, 96, 97, 118, 120:
Christopher Horwood

p. 16 (below): Halip Studio

pp. 20-21: portraits of Sir John Vanbrugh, John Carr
and Sir Thomas Robinson: National Portrait Gallery

p. 23 (above left): courtesy of Philip Howard

pp. 27, 101 (above): Granada Television and the
Estate of Evelyn Waugh

p. 28: Board of Trustees of the Victoria and Albert Museum

p. 34 (above): *The Yorkshire Post*

pp. 36-39: The antiquities on display, courtesy
of the National Museums Liverpool

pp. 39 (below), 54: Mattia Aquila

pp. 42, 75 (below), 128 (above): Peter Smith Photography

pp. 49, 52 (above): *Country Life*

p. 66: courtesy Chatto & Windus

p. 69 (above): courtesy of Tate Britain

p. 95 (top right): Charlotte Graham; p. 95 (all others): Tom Arber

p. 101 (below): courtesy of Netflix © 2020 Netflix INC

pp. 108, 109, 114, 115: Tony Whittaker

p. 110: by kind permission of Sir Andrew Morritt;
photograph Eddie Ryle-Hodges

p. 132 (left): Graham Ella / Alamy Stock Photo

p. 133 (below): courtesy of the Environment Bank

Christopher Ridgway has been curator at Castle Howard
since 1984. He is Chair of the Yorkshire Country House
Partnership and Professor in the Centre for the Study of
Historic Irish Houses and Estates. He has lectured extensively
on Castle Howard's collections and history.

The floorplan for Vanbrugh's house as it appeared in *Vitruvius Britannicus* in 1715. Today the footprint of the house is different.

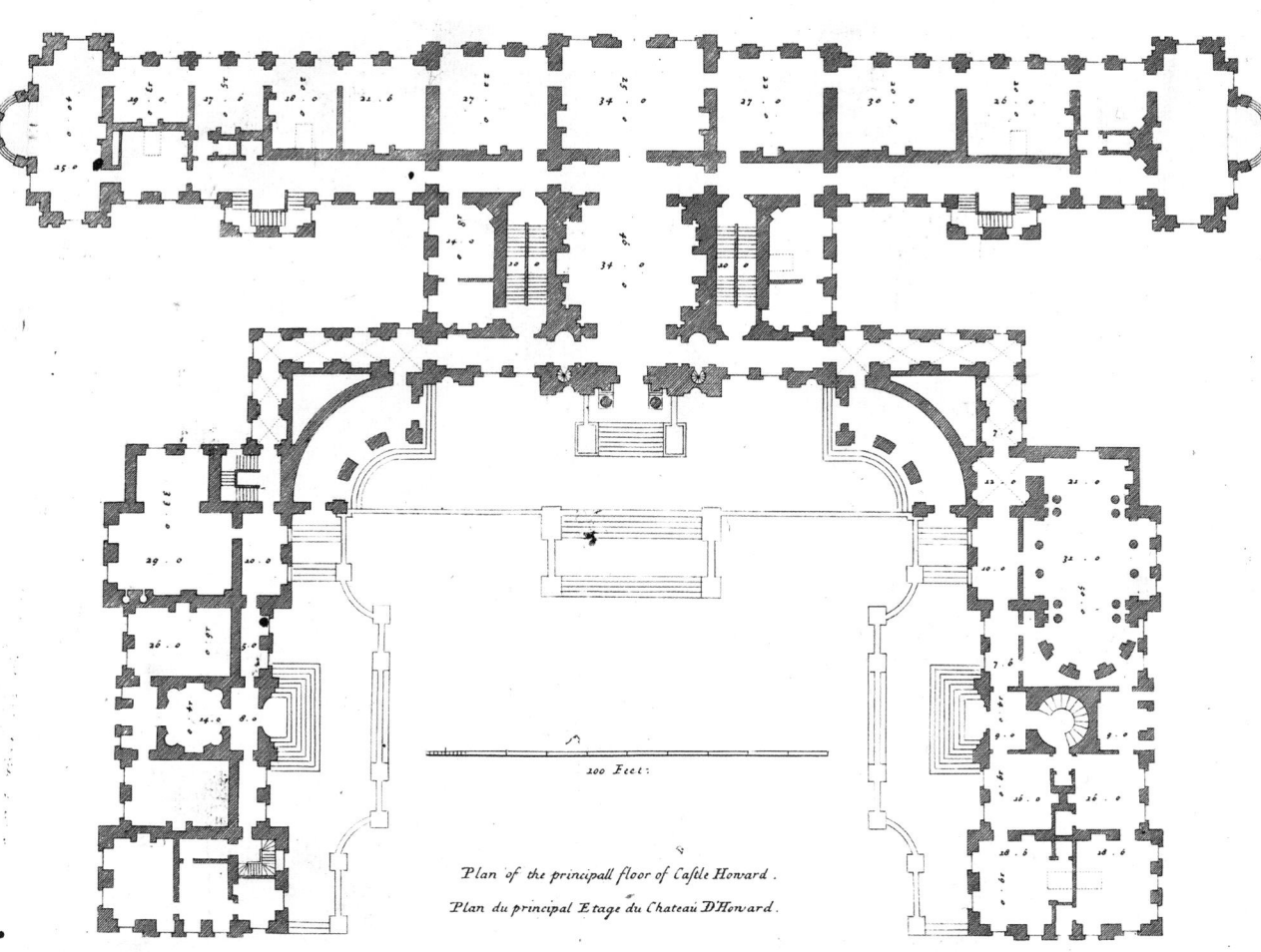

100 Feet:

Plan of the principall floor of Castle Howard.

Plan du principal Etage du Chateau D'Howard.